+/-*

+/-*

Minimi Opera

ἐπώνυμος mūtātiōnēs

÷

Eponymous transformations

Opérations éponymes

N·A·N·K·E

© 2015, Edmond-Aimé Kabushemeye Nkinzo.

+ / -*

Though alienating and frightening I maintain the hope and the vision that whatever I do, now, amounts only to small accomplishments, compared to what I need to do in the future.

My duty simply entails to do what is within my power where no one has the will to do what must be done.

• •

J'étais, je suis et je serai la même personne. Je suis le changement mais aussi tant la cause que le résultat. Toutes ces opérations sont éponymes à mon âme.

• • • • • • • • • • • • • • • • • • •

·•·•·•··•·•··•·•··•·•··•·•··•·•·

+ / -*

En cherchant des inspirations, j'espère que j'en inspire

Par accident, dans l'occident, j'inhale de l'oxygène
Je me libère de ma peine et bientôt je le fais sans gène
Sur quelques lignes et quelques points sans dimensions
Juste assez pour garder la tête haute pendant l'immersion

Mon sort m'est inconnu
Mais je pense à l'avance à des décennies
Sachant bien que j'y serai décédé

Je ne suis que semence prise dans le feu de la passion

Serais-je comme plusieurs
Un homme d'un siècle de deux jours?
Où seuls la naissance et la mort prennent court
Où se ruent des bêtes rouées de coups
Dans de cruels duels à l'ombre de sombres ruelles
Qui naissent et meurent à quatre pattes
En pleurant et en bêlant car les mots perdent leur court?

Quel serait le poids d'un livre
Si je ne mettais pas le monde sur du papier?
Ce monde qui mène plusieurs à en rêver d'autres.
Rien d'étonnant que ces rêves persistent
Car ce monde ci ne prend pas fin non plus

Quoi qu'on en dise je vagabonde ici et là sans me perdre
Entre des contrées divisées par quelques devises
Alors que je rêve de mon du

Je suis un peu mal parti et mal pris
Mais je m'y mets et paie le prix.
Bien que désabonné des nouvelles
J'ignore ce que coûte la vie ici-bas
Mais tu m'en diras plus quand tu mendieras

+ / - *

Malgré soi, plusieurs nous aimeront
Même si on pense les en empêcher

Même si cela n'en a pas l'air
Même si je parle avec un soupçon de colère
Néanmoins, malgré moi, malgré tout, je parle d'amour

Je brise la glace, en attendant un hiver doux
De peur que je me retrouve coincé en-dessous
Dans l'une de nombreuses missives
Qui par amour ont pris la forme de poèmes

Les mots en surface font du surplace
De peur de les perdre, je les compte, les épelles
Les roule et les déroule, les emmêle et les démêle

Que ce soit au sujet d'exquises esquisses d'esclaves à une escale
De caricatures de colosses derrière les coulisses
D'un vide qui ne laisse aucune trace
Ou de l'empreinte indélébile de la crasse
J'ignore comment je m'y prends mais j'en suis sûr
Certains vers sortent après que je les mesure

Mais à jamais étourdi, à peu près peu après
Je verse deux verres et puis catastrophe
J'inverse des vers sur quatre strophes

Faut-il donc que soit maudit ceux que le ciel n'a pas bénit?
J'approche le ciel, mais indécis, l'enfer aussi

Au bout du compte
Je saigne par la rime
Je me soigne et je signe

• • • • • • • • • • • • • • • • •

+ / -*

Here implied are the implications of the imperative

I don't waste my time with the past.
If I only needed to wait for tomorrow
I could settle down
But I've set up a couple of dates
With destiny throughout this century

Due to the green light
Given for yellow lines
In that rum red tape
Many of my stars died
A long time ago
But in the distance
I get to see them again

Traveling with extant light from extinguished fires
The past is always present

Lulled as I indulge in dull delight
I get close enough for comfort
Soon, I faintly hear an incipient storm
That reminds me of the growl of a waking beast
As the night rises in the east

It's not that I don't think I have the time
I just don't think the timing is right

I'm the paragon of procrastinating
But when I think of dying
Without doing certain things I get going

I'm sorry if it's not what I promised you to do

Odd habits foster odd skills
So I end up killing time with things time kills

+ / -*

Thanks to strong impressions made in short times
I started flocking with birds with the weirdest feathers
But this way all that gets thrown at me I can weather

Though we hanged high
I pondered on hypotheses brought to me by hypoxia
Yet, too loose, the noose released me

I realized late that I went ahead of myself
And ended at the same place
Because in the beginning
There was nowhere to go

Praying to a trinity in haikus
I saw my prey behind golden gates
And started moving the pliers.
I hope I don't get caught because I have priors

Life is the only sensation I am trying to make sense of
This one, the next one or the lack thereof

Some mornings I wake up like one escapes a prison
And I breathe in
As though I wasn't breathing
And maybe I wasn't

Though proudly bigger on the inside
I lay powerless in wait of a power up.
I am nervous, waiting for the universe
To give me the next verse

Unphased by the barks of dogs
That bounced back from the bark of trees
I hear clearly their voices crack while breaking under the ax
Yet I intend to cut even deeper
I aim to enter the paper and pull out a poem

+/-*

It is my careless craving for carving and creating

While taking steps towards infinity
With the feeling of wanting something out reach
Poetry became my way of honing language
To make my mother tongue
The one of my sisters and my brothers
And keep a record of each of my transformations

I am always trying to come up with a better come back
Because I know it always comes down
To getting back up and getting right back

I cannot just build up a rap sheet
And end up slamming in the slammer.
I must know how much I can do before I go to jail

Whatever one can do
Is gonna have to do

That's the long and short of it

With my voice out there
I am listening for echoes and resonance
Proofs of boundaries and room for growth
Which is why I started out quite quiet
But I quit that real quick

I was not here
Yet these are my words
Now, I am

•·•·•··•·•··•·•··•·•··•·•·

+ /_*

Poems/Poèmes

+ / _*

Poetica

+ / -*

XIX

The hope, the hype, the high

Sono già un padre

Ogni giorno, lei cresce un po di più
Dimenticando ieri come un sogno
E sogno di lei. So già che sara la mia gioia
La sua anima gioca ancora la su, nel celo blu.
Con un sorriso puro, mi riconoscerà un giorno.
Lei aspetta ancora con la sua madre, la mia piccina

Higashi no Hana (The thirst and the struggle, they're real)

I complain at times that people don't believe me
But often enough I am unbelievable

My paraphrasing comes from the parallax
Of the digital ink running in parallel
To the line under my pen.
I urge my index over the tablet
To inscribe symbols that come forth
From my humble appreciation
Of the overflowing energy
That wells up in me to finally spill on paper

In the middle of a pandemonium
I am the paragon of a man
In pursuit of happiness and purpose

I ponder over the pother in my mind
Puzzled by the need to choose
One of my many conflicting paradigms

I traded life force for light speed
To get a couple of years closer to my goals
But now I worry remembering misplacing a stick in the forest

Out of the deadly sins I practiced all seven
I paid heed to the head of the heathens.
He spoke of many things and had me fooled
With just a few things strewed over greater lengths.
In the premise of terrifying omens
He was the most pious of ravens

Yet I turned red crossing the Rubicon
When asked by a foreign land to stand in for a scion
Because I dream of coming from another world

I go again through the same old things, now just older
And the gimmick becomes a rhythmic rut
That is taught to runts
Until they rot in the rule if they do not riot

Though it's incredible to some that I would inquire so
Must the cradle be a crucible?
I wear a pendant akin to a crucifix
But I cross my heart attempting to fix
The need for a fluke as specified in the specs
Made by sparse paupers
People of power that are now spectres

Though they say it's hard to stay faithful
The leap can be uplifting
And if you bothered to count your blessings
Instead of your problems
Then you would know of the 99 names.
So don't waste your time trying to change neighbours
When you cannot change your home

Similarly, I was wondering if she would have me
But I confess it's not the first time
That I try to get into heaven.
She put me through hell so maybe we are even

+/-*

I would blow kisses
Aiming at her slender body like blowing at embers
Looking to light a tall fire
In the eye of the storm in her heart

She would tell me that I think she's the worst
But I would often think of her
And I never thought so

I am in my element where I feel adamant.
The sparks in the air might light the powder
While I try to make stronger bonds.
In the pursuit of happiness, I attempt black magic

I am trying to conceive of how much she can receive
Out of all that I can give
And though I ask that she appreciates this incomplete rendition
Because like life, beautiful things need not end
To gain a sizeable value
And though some things may be cut to size
I seize this moment, I am a sieve
Looking for atonement with tricks up my sleeves
To gain the upper hand
And if she cannot forgive me
I hope she comes to understand
Because time vindicates
What one doesn't appreciate but appreciates

Will I reach gravitas
Before gravity pulls me to my grave?
I prepare the counter of cremation
Hoping that when the wind blows right
I will be mixed in with it
And there will be nothing left

My gamble

I caught myself in a hurry
Hunting for a red herring

I thought in sales my numbers could only rise
But the wind in my sails had me realize
That they can keep the words and take the digits.
My hands shorten and I feel my limits
I get a few tickets printed for some visits
But join other hermits in the last minutes

Yet I take steps with fervour
At times forgetting my place
Trying to go a bit further

My gamble is
To have my mother tongue accentuated
Even if she sits on tongues that underestimate it
To leave no topics uncovered
In the few things I dare say I discovered
To move forward regardless of profits
To fall back again in a poet's habits
Of unadulterated joys of youth
That made me stubborn and aloof

Serein et souverain

Pour la haine que l'on me porte
Certains sautent par la fenêtre

On me dit suspect mais c'est surprenant
Car ça sous-entend que je suis en suspension
Et que les suspicions à mon égard
N'ont pas encore de raison
Et je m'abstiens car l'absolution
N'est absolument pas ma solution

Je ne me vois que de passage
Mais, déjà, je m'en vais voir le passeur
Alors j'envisage d'entailler les âges
Sans consulter de tailleur

Je marche la nuit, enduit de cambouis
Pas moins avide que les gens dans ces bolides
Et comme sur une terre aride
Ma soif presse mon pas
Et je brûle de désir
Pour des plaisirs dont je ne me souviens pas

Ce n'est que la fin de la semaine
Mais le début de mes tracas
Je m'y attache un peu trop et passe au dessert
Trois quart d'un verre et je me retrouve à terre

A call for unrest (in times of peace)

Discover, disagree, disbelieve
Disappoint, disapprove, disuade

Disgrace, disillusion
Disenchant, distort

Disengage, disarm
Disband, disassociate
Disconnect, disperse

Disobey, dishonour, disfavour

Disrobe, display
Discharge, disturb
Disgust, disrupt

Dismissed

A dark horse of a rain

I was tired and I was hurt
But I figured I had to go back out
I needed to do something
I had to go get something
Had to watch something
Read something
Something...

I waited a bit thinking I could make it
I didn't realize I was still so sensitive
To the sound of rain pouring out.
I thought it wouldn't get to me
While I laid far from my window
But it did and instead I slept half a day

I underestimated the rain

I let myself go

My vision was pulsating
From the subtle throb of my body.
I was alive, with bated breath.
I was leaning backwards
Both feet on that ledge.
I forget how I took a wrong turn.
I forget how I fell from that height
Not much, not nothing
And yet I managed to bring it down
My shame, my warmth

I let myself go

Je me débrouille

On ne sait jamais ce qu'on devient
Et quand on s'en souvient
Notre tout n'est déjà plus rien
On change vite de chemin
Le pas léger et l'esprit serein
Toujours un jour d'ici à demain

Je rugis brièvement avant de joindre le reste de la jungle
Et mon cœur cogne dans les creux de mon corps
Mais je croîs avec mon cran qui boit d'un écrin
Et j'écris mes maux et les relis maintes fois à l'écran

Je parle assez la langue de l'amour
Pour inscrire des mots sur ta peau
Pour poser des lettres sur tes pavillons
Pour fredonner des chansons dans tes souvenirs

Je ne suis pas un expert et je n'ai pas d'exploits
Je suis d'ailleurs maladroit et je risque de ne pas faire le poids
Mais de peur que tu me files entre les doigts
À chaque fois, je me faufile
Jusqu'au début de la file
Qui mène vers toi

+ /_*

La vie en enfer

Quoi qu'on en dise ma gourmandise retient mon avarice
C'est avec orgueil que je dépense mon oseille
Je me luxe le poignet en guise de luxure
Ma colère s'intensifie pour les cons
Et ma paresse progresse avec d'étranges envies

Conscient de mon cancer
Je cherche à poser mon ancre
Là où je déverse mes vers
Sous forme de verres d'encre
Au milieu de mes lacunes
Maintenant devenus lacs
Où se reflète ma lune
Et je pousse au loin ma peine
Le temps que mon soleil les sèche
Le temps que me monte l'eau aux yeux
Et bien que je le sache
Je choisis d'en ignorer les raisons
Car mon cœur ne me rejoint plus
Là où vont mes idées ...

La vie en enfer...
Faute de sursis, je commence à m'y faire
Et quand j'en jouis, je pense à en faire

La visite

J'entends encore mes extrémités froisser les draps
Le vent bouger les rideaux contre la fenêtre
Les pas qui faisaient craquer le plancher
Ses habits s'entasser au sol
La lune entrer dans la chambre.
On devint quelque chose de sombre
Et dans les décombres de ce qui fut détruit en cette nuit là
Girent nos corps immobiles
Après qu'ils aient dansé
Comme les offrandes pour un feu
Qui nous consumait à l'accoutumée.
Je me rappelle comment je questionnais mes désirs
Le nombre de jour où je l'ai convoitée sans la toucher
La façon dont on évitait le sujet
Mais aussi dont on se comprenait
En parlant de tout autre chose.
Nos langues roses parlaient déjà un dialecte commun
Alors quand elles se touchaient, on se comprenait
Parmi des mots mâchés et des soupirs saccadés

A bit of your splendor

I caught on to a bit of your candor
And my move was not at all clever.
I foresaw you giving me the cold shoulder
But your hand warmed mine
And our sin saw light
From the shroud of darkness we had worn
And though our bond is now torn
Each time that was a first
Managed to linger and last

In the shade of a camphor tree looking for comfort
I used an unofficial format for the rewrite
Of a letter I sent you so we could have a word.
You mean the world to me
And the world means nothing without you
Because I caught on to a bit of your splendor

De pensées en pansements

La colère nous rend capable de beaucoup de cruauté

Son cœur rugissait dans ma main
Quand j'empoignais ses seins

Il fallait que je me soigne du désir de sa peau.
Je n'ai pas la bonne attitude
Mais c'est que ce n'est pas dans mes habitudes
De vivre autant de clichés de suite
Et de retomber dans la platitude

J'aurais voulu qu'elle m'accompagne
Qu'elle laisse tout tomber et me rejoigne en campagne
Qu'elle n'ait rien d'autre et laisse tomber son pagne
Qu'elle me rende fou et devienne ma compagne

Moi je me méfis de sa peau
Mais j'en fais fis comme un sot
Je connais sa croix et son fardeau
Mais je mets la main au feu et me jette à l'eau
Oui sans soucis je fais le saut
Même si sans sursis j'ai des sursauts
Et comme je le soupçonnais, un soupçon de plaisir
Permet à sa fleur de s'épanouir

Je sais que je n'ai pas de peau
Je ne sais jamais quand c'est faux.
Il fait déjà si chaud
Je n'avais rien sur les os mais là j'en ai mis trop

Je cours de plaies en plaisirs mais de pensées en pansements
Je dépense bien trop et passe trop de mon temps
A panser mes plaies en me remplissant la panse
Pour mettre autre chose là où se dessine son absence

+/-*

Draft poet (The gatherer)

Lately I've been into street authors, artists and chemists
That have been writing on the side of the streets
With grafittis and bodies
Unwritten laws depicted with all their flaws

Like me, my poetry comes in pieces.
Puzzling as it may seem I am just guessing
How to put my life and my words together
Stringing along a long line of thoughts
Unravelling simplicity into its intrinsic complexity
Exposing how chaos sits in the margins of order
With words that may be reordered, appended and removed
From the original work that keeps grinding in my ear
And as the cogs stumble in movement
I marvel at the translations
The harmonious movement in between
Languages, cultures and paradigms
Of ubiquitous elements in the realm of men

It might seem a bit daft
But I dabble so little in light of the dark
Even this is only a draft

Thus I have been a dense dunce
Waiting on a dance
Feeling smaller and smaller
And I spun around
With a heart pulsating
To the beat of hydrogen clocks
And now I comb through the people
With my eyes until they meet yours
And I make them stand until I let go of them
And reach for the sky

In a slow hurry

Things got a bit hairy
And now I am in a hurry
But the faster I go
The slower and the deeper I feel things.
As though not to miss a thing
It all slows down as I speed up.
My heart feels light
As my mind heavy with worry enters a fight
To keep up with things relative to it.
The destination still feels far
For the speed doesn't erase the distance

Like moving between realities
I recall fragments of a future I haven't chosen yet.
I shake to speak the truth and start to fret

Which worlds are true?
I fall, many times, black and blue.
Storming into an unfair fight
I fear to be defining my sight in this light
Caught in the rules of games still playing.
I reel on a string ending on a red herring.
I attempt an escape but it extends my stay

Like the dreams I have come out of each day
Maybe I just have to reach the limits of this life
Maybe I must hurdle my body into its boundaries
In an unending and sorrowful strife
Pursuing richer and fuller planes of existence

+ / -*

L'enfant perdue (C'est la voisine)

Quand elle pense au reste de sa vie
Elle pense à une ville
Elle n'y voit rien qui vaille
Mais c'est que tout lui est vil.
Elle se perd déjà sur sa voie
Et lorsqu'elle perd tout de vue
Ses appels au secours s'en vont avec sa voix.
Elle ne parle déjà plus
Elle danse de nuit, elle plane de jour
Elle reçoit des sous de porcs
Elle nourrit de vieux vautours.
Les yeux ouverts dans le noir, elle dort

Sa compagnie ...
Elle n'est plus avare
Elle est maintenant avide
Et ça l'aide à ne pas voir qu'elle est vide
Voire qu'elle ne va nulle part.
Elle vadrouille entre quelques ruelles
Pour de petites morts qui la font survivre d'une façon cruelle.
Elle vaque et vogue dans des mers anciennes
Et les vagues subtiles la mènent vers de vastes terres arides.
Elle n'est qu'un vase pour une seule fleur fanée
Refusée par le seul homme qu'elle aimait

On a eu un vigil pour elle il y a vingt ans.
C'était la voisine et vite fait
Pris sur le vif, ils prirent ses effets.
Ses parents le virent trop tard.
Son envol hier fut son dernier.
Elle ne visait pas si haut
Elle ne voulait que brièvement planer
Mais on ne voulait pas d'elle là-haut

+ / -*

Pixelated Early Monday Service (Primordial Extra-Marital Sex)

I spit grit on her spitting image
Made easy on the eye
Because she weighs heavy on my mind

Melting inside the torrid forge of my passions
I plunge to my ruin

Must she taste this heavenly?
My sin is to sense her thoroughly

I dabble in the mother tongue
Of her ancestry adrift in history.
I only touch the walls of her city
And I can feel her getting closer
In a slow waltz of seraphim feathers
Behind a curtain of cinders

But I have concerns about how she concerted her own demise
Surrounding herself with hideous hearts of jealous hydras
Fussing and fighting over a quick fix for feisty foxes

She plays me as she plies me with words.
I played it off well as I took off her plaid clothing

I am really not that bright
Must we really turn off the light?
We are in hot water
But I am really not that deep, I don't follow
Can she swim down though I make myself a bit shallow?

I fell for her but now I feel hollow.
I swear her name among a few I should hallow

+/-*

I rolled the dice and spread the dye
And as I dialed, something died.
In the evidence I found innocence.
Both are gone and now it makes sense

She needs to make love to find any.
She needs it bad even if it's this bad
But all the honey has to do is bear this.

I leave the monopoly of monotony with monogamies.
I am a savage without a savior
And what I cannot salvage I will savour

+/-*

The matter of energy (Spectrum)

A lot goes in living a little for people with no life
But the dead dread the idea of dwelling where strife is rife

Slipping through the sluices of my closed third eye
My vision cascades in the last shade of blurry cataracts
And I retract my adulations at the sound of the bank
Of a body of water that contracts
And the reverberation of souls that impact
Where matter and energy meet and attract
Where laws are exacted and freedom is exulted.
I rehearse tracts of facts on the acts of fat cats
But lose track of those distracted by the version redacted.
Still, I reacted when the inverse was made law and enacted
And though my intelligence was insulted
I entertained the idea before it was rejected

I strained my body trying to attain
Something that pertains to perpetuity
Looking for a way to make matter
Reach the depths of infinity through energy
But I failed to find sources of untapped resources in my vicinity.
I was still afraid of losing myself to nature and its complexity

When I learned how to read a flame
I learned that I too could burn bright
And when I heard of different temperatures in it
I started wondering which colors I was emitting out
From within the dark canvas of the cold cosmos

I hum a few hertz close
To the closing connection with the planet
Trying to hold on an equilibrium
In the infinite span of my spectrum

+/-*

I feel a throb rob me of calm.
My heart pounds my ribcage and oscillates my body.
I realize my life is at first subtle continuous motions
Of a muscle that rocks my very core
And this is the most natural wave I can send out
I emit it constantly

Attesting to my nature I find new ways to function
Finding myself again and again locked
In the embrace of a sentence
From a cosmic and comic poem that I can only utter
When I add lyrics to the melody that rings in the shape of life

Is it too farfetched for me to reach
For that next stretch of thread of chaos
In the tapestry of order
As I back away bringing beauty into focus?

I tug and pull and with one more push outwards
I feel the resilience of the nexus
On the shackles that make my worldly bonds

La Preuve (la peur)

Si je devais attendre que le soleil se couche
Je me réveillerais pendant la nuit, de l'eau à la bouche
Alors je suppose qu'il fait déjà nuit
Et je me réveille au clair de la lune

Dans le vide de la nuit
J'écoute le subtil bruit
Des dernières émissions
Sur des fréquences qui s'en vont

Ce sont les détails des voix
De mes proches qui s'éteignent

Comme ma vue, mon ouïe disparait
Une note à la fois
Et mes autres sens les accompagnent.
Bientôt je serai seul avec mes pensées
Et ces absurdités prendront le dessus

En cherchant le silence
Je commence par des mots vides de sens
Et puis j'écris les notes
Que je remplace par des pauses
Et le papier se vide

Je vois s'empirer mes symptômes.
Je n'écris plus que pour un fantôme
Que quelques mirages avant le glaucome

Le prestige de vestiges vétustes
Se forme quand je ne peux pas
Terminer une œuvre.
Je mets longtemps la main sur la planche
Avant que je me désoeuvre

+ / _*

Je ferme les yeux et un son soutenu
Dessine dans ma tête une image continue

Loin des pécores sur des parapets
Devenues pimbêches au panache inspiré de pot-pourri
Je me penche sur l'idée d'avoir un enfant
Et sur sa future mère en l'embrassant

Je m'enlise au milieu de fils de soie
Je prie et me cous à ma croix
Et du coup, je plis et je n'ai plus froid.
Je rêve à nouveau d'elle.
Mes trêves, de jour, ne durent pas

Je suis une victime de mes passions
De la rime et de l'induction
D'une ivresse fugace et d'un besoin vorace
Et ce qui m'est singulier c'est qu'en particulier
Je trouve puéril plusieurs de ses pourriels
Où l'homme au pluriel la punit en étant partiel

Je confesse être fasciné par la fiction
Que je confectionne autour de l'affection
Que je falsifie et que je façonne

Je marmonne quelques excuses de peur que l'on me comprenne
Mais avec l'espoir que l'on me pardonne

Je fais attention depuis que j'ai entendu
Qu'il y a une tension dans ses sous-entendus

Je lis entre les lignes de ses vêtements
Je connais le secret de ses mouvements

J'abuse et j'ose exagérer au sujet d'exégèses.
Je devine faute d'hypothèses
Et je nous anticipe déjà aux antipodes dans mon antithèse

J'arbore l'idée de m'esquisser une échappatoire
Et je garde, pour moi, les murmures
Que je fais dans cet observatoire
Et comme l'étoile qu'elle joue dans ma fiction
Elle n'est plus que le feu éteint sur une toile noire
Si distante que je crois la voir luire

C'est ce qui m'échappe qui me tourmente
Mais me garde dans son étreinte
J'en récite les consignes et ma voix s'éreinte.
Il ne me reste de mes quelques plaies que des plaintes
Parsemées dans quelques scènes bientôt peintes

Si je pouvais expliquer ce qui m'habite
Je saurais comment fonder une famille
Mais je ne suis que le moine qui se déshabille.
Je ne suis pas habile mais j'en fait part de façon explicite

Si elle m'écoute, sans doute
Elle sait ce que me coûte
Chacune de ses larmes qui ont coulé.
Je prie le ciel qu'un jour
Je trouve une preuve, même par l'absurde
Pour donner raison à mon corps de bouger malgré ma peur
Et de mettre un de mes genoux, à ses pieds, à terre

Le pire c'est que je fais de mon mieux quand néanmoins
Comme un abruti je n'aboutis à rien

+ / -*

Solely in advisory capacity (Just saying)

Unsurpassed in my passion I found my compass
In my pastime spent on passwords on my passage
And over the underpass I heard the word I inhabit
And when I pass on I hope I pass on my spirit

From a boon to bane and now a bore at the bar
I too was thrown out of kilter when my ship was scuppered.
Looking from afar through doors ajar, I was bewildered
At the crafting of cruft sifted into a spate of hearts black as tar

When you are not the same person anymore
You will understand who you were before.
You will have changed when the invariable looks different

Let me illuminate you on the light
That shines from those lucifers
And the reckless disregard from the colossus
Stepping on the delicate balance
Through loopholes and the pontification of assholes

Some don't have to play their hand to get the upper hand
Even when they only have one turn left
In the game to make a stand

No one in their right mind
Wouldn't change their mind
But much is brought to obsolescence
When a people is beaten into obedience
But if complaining works out for you
You really cannot complain

Now, if you may extend your patience …

Once a vigilante

I came back in time just to avoid time travel.
I go for the hands of time to grab yours in mine
But if I had loved u sooner
Would I have loved u longer
And would it be any better? I wonder

I knight myself with a strange knife
And start the slow build to a silly strife
Something that I hope can keep the memory of your life

I have to stay out of the yellow lines
But I fall with a yellow fever
And my fear turns into a yellow taint.
I feel a fire but the distance makes it faint.
I fall short with my sins but I work to be a saint

As though the sentinels had no sentiments
About the sentence of those on the fence
I hear the gates of my heaven close behind you
And I can tell that I am now going to live in hell

With the sigil of a sibyl
I thought of joining the vigil
But I harbored ill will
So I became a vigilante
Prolific to proponents and opponents

Hanging with high class low lives
Soon I am more jaded than jazzed
But it could only come across as crass
As I feel the need to cross the people on this crescent

Drowning in inaudible dialogue
Looking for spots with pots to piss in

+ / -*

We were told to piss off .
We spoke of peace
For those resting
While the living kept running.

Dazed for days, minding the prospect of prosperity
While we mined without a canary into austerity
Allegedly I was lost in logical legerdemain
While my ledger was bleeding red.
Though I should go back into black
I ended each time back in bed

Where does my time go?
I tire myself into sleeping
But never lie and never wake

Surely I should fathom
The surly bonds of fate
Facing my failures
To reach enlightenment
And break my bondage

I have been moving forward while putting things behind me.
I had to move in and out just to move on
And naturally I made some irregular moves
While facing the music
In public performances of humanity that became therapeutic

+ / -*

The antebellum

I have been taking stabs at a few things
But things are never clear cut.
I had to give it one try just trusting my gut
That I wouldn't fall flat on my face.
I was not in shape so I wouldn't fall with grace

In the background, a Zathura soundtrack record

To my gentle Azazel
To my fierce Jezebel
To my dear Elizabeth
To my queen Zenobia

When it hit me, I was eating my size of zizania in a plaza.
I had to show that I was enough zealous
To bring azaleas and zinnias for her credenza
And zircon for her first month, our first month
So I headed to a bazaar
And there, in my zone
I was zapped with a zax

You share your zeta azimuth
With the sun at the zenith
So I should accompany a few stanzas with a cadenza.
It's typical of people with my zodiac sign
To storm into hazard attracting buzzards
But I have the pizzazz of a wizard
And I showed up holding my hands in the form of a peziza

Though we were grounded in fear of flight
From some silly strife and an insipid slight
We had our first fight before our first night
But we made right before the first light

+/-*

I remember the dread in light of sheer blight
I can recall my eyes regaining sight

Now I see the struggle comes as we sit tight
Treating as trite something that won't kill us but might
Just because we pulled through things with more might

But something was not right.
Did I mistake a battle for a war
Because I didn't want to fight anymore?
Will you open up once more like before?
My hands are already sore from being hit by the door

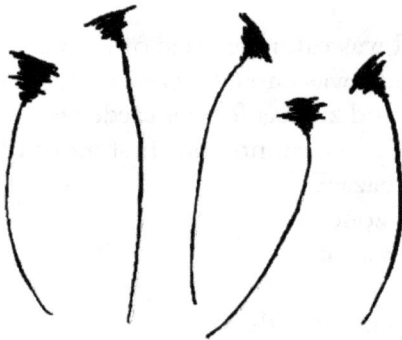

Quelques de mes voeux

Chaque matin me rappelle ton penchant pour les petits pains
Les petits pois et ton appétit pour les petits plats

Je n'imagine toujours pas le pire
Car c'est mieux pour moi quand on est ensemble

Je n'ai pas de peau quand je ne suis pas près de toi
Je reprends mon poste aussi vite que je peux.
Je ne suis pauvre que quand on n'est pas à deux
Même si on ne finit par ne gagner que des prunes

Ça m'a surpris, sur le vif, paf, sur le pif et plouf dans l'eau
J'ai appris comment ton visage était un présage en vue d'orages
Comme un oracle mais sans aucun miracle

Je ne savais pas combien tu avais souffert
Je ne pouvais que te souffler des mots moins amers.
Et puis j'y pense, qu'aurais-je pu faire à l'époque?
On était paralysés par la peur mais on persistait quand même

Le passage piéton était trop périlleux
Alors on courut pour sauter à pieds joins
Un peu plus loin sur le pied de terre

Tu ne bougeais plus, tu voulais rester parterre
De peur de ne plus avoir les pieds sur terre
Et tu faisais du pouce des deux bras.
Tu ne serais allée nulle part
Et j'avais peur que ce soit sans moi

Je cherche à maitriser la leçon
Je veux apprendre comment vivre avec toi
Mais je ne sais pas si je ferai le poids

+/-*

Je ne sais pas ce qui me pique
Mais des fois il arrive que je m'applique.
Je te venais au secours
Alors que je n'en connaissais pas le tour.
Je ne suis qu'un page
Sur ces quelques vers.
Je ne tournerais la page
Que quand ma plume y versera des verres

Je me prépare mais trop se passe
Et parfois je suis dépassé

Je voyais le pourtour s'empresser de nous prendre
Dans une étreinte mortelle
Et pourtant j'étais partant

Je me retrouve souvent pêle-mêle
Cherchant comment te dire que tu es belle
Même quand la peine peint ta poisse sur ta frimousse

Je n'avais pas compris à quel point
On pouvait se sacrifier
Pour quelqu'un que l'on connait à peine
Mais je connais la peine
De ne pas connaitre quelqu'un
Et de saigner à force de serrer les poings

Je n'ai aucune pitié pour toi, que de l'amitié
Que de l'amour, que ma sincérité

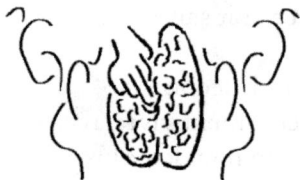

Pedantry and Glossolalia in Love Proclamations (Breakdown)

Barreling into barren worlds, life barely makes it

I am now here from nowhere

I am a dummy; I can crash into my crush
When my ideas become concrete.
I break into laughter when I try to remain discrete
But suddenly I realize I lost yet another half of myself

I gave my heart to one who had a hand in me losing my head
And now for a shorthand I make a handstand with my pen
And I only pull a homerun when I pull a Homer

My heart will only beat a certain number of times
Making it go faster will only shave time off my life
And I will be cashing out with cachexia

But I'm still not out of the woods
Soon with minutes in the afternoon
I will think of the moon

I have a bachelor with minor faults in my major theory
So I was sent to the slaughter for a slight at the masters

Our chemistry could be broken down
Into essential elements of any relationship out there
Our chemistry could be broken up
By all the little things we let in from elsewhere
But it won't suffice to add the -ism suffix
To make an isthmus between the two of us.
If the sea quells the seagulls
Then I can go for the sequel
And dive further than what is said to be lethal

+/-*

Waiting on the cosign from her zodiac sign
I withdrew on the bank of a river
To strike into stone the swan song of our stars that align
And sculpt the salient shape of the spear of a sinner

I am now afraid to mention how she got my attention.
I have trouble on my mind when I think of her
She is the focus of this feeling
That I try to restore but start to distort

Looking for a lens for my third eye
Though I like my blurred vision and don't know why
I close my eyes often to take in what I magnify
And when I can't stand it or take it, I just lie

I am stretching the tether to my mind
Letting myself get higher

We come from higher places so we seek elevation
And being grounded is a mortal condition
That doesn't resemble our original disposition

I don't know if she could ever understand
Taking concrete vacations because of something abstract
Like the extract left in our genes
From kings and queens of the motherland

Aimless and endless, the curb thins the gap before the axis
But theorizing too long can be a disservice to the practice
So excuse me, if I go in unprepared

Fire grinds my body into ashes
The heavy smoke hangs for a while in the air
Before it travels and dilutes further than I ever went
But there are places where my guts tell me not to go to
For my soul would not be able to leave them

+ / -*

When I had that feeling about her side, I rushed to it

At first like novices with a clutter of devices
Convinced of some sort of breakthrough
We spent nights awake talking about the smallest things.
We spoke of the craziest things
Among which stood out "love" and "forever"
Yet flat out, I was told of bumps on the road
And my blimp in the sky would meet with thunder
My boat on the sea would go under
And my plans on this earth would go asunder.
My life flashes with a reel of bloopers and blunders
And I look blind when I stumble on this path of wonders

Lucky me, I caught her silhouette exit a waterfall
Where I was practicing drowning and downfall.
Her feet disappeared in the gradient
Of the foam and her immaculate dress
And I feared that like a mermaid of ancient Greece
She would make me drown
But foolish as I was I just walked up to her
Trying to remember how long
I could hold my breath underwater
All the while, in the depth of her eyes
My mind had already sunk deeper than any ocean.
I reached with my lips on the port of her words
And dug my own grave further

As I scratched the surface of her mystery
The dress unravelled and I realized that she was Calypso
She was the sea, she was a woman, she was the deep
She was the waves, she was the cycles, she was life

+/-*

Perfunctory thirst

I must inform you that my work is experimental in form.
What I am aiming for is far out of range
And when I hit that spot I expect the winds to change

I was but across them when it hit me
That the last straw was a draw
Between my expression
And how I expressed in my drawings
Streaks of losses and the express need
To draw a couple of crosses

We don't know anything
Yet we go through every day
Hanging onto an undeniable truth.
We do not freeze in front of the staggering unknown
And most of us will humble themselves in temples
While others stumble at the steps leading to stables
Trying to live faster
Aware of the little time we have
But feeling so close to the end
Feeling so close to the edge

That too is approaching infinity

Yet discrete with my errors
My imperfection started to grow
With the decay in the illusion they painted me in

Intense care has been taken for me to get into remission
But I failed to go further than what allowed the admission

I go about bouts and whereabouts
About barks on bark and bites

+/-*

I have dreams of a sleepless city
With bloodshot eyes trying to glean at a glimpse of the present
While the past lingers on my nerves
And keeps the mind reminiscent

Must we increase the complexity
To keep completeness and integrity?

Leave a comic with a comment
And he will pull the cosmic out of a comet

There is bound to be a frantic romantic at the frontiers.
The horizon and the green grass give the mind a free pass

Despite death, life should be an early respite
Making a living out of making a killing
But the order breaks anything that breaks the order
So it came down to me
Waiting for the come up
A day where I would come to
And find that I have come through

+ / -*

Something to write home about (Letters in the -male)

I spent my last dollar today
All my credit cards are over the limit
I owe even more to friends and family
I stretched the hand I was given all the way
I even inched for a few miles more
But I was shut down at the door.
I open my fridge and my milk went bad
The eggs I bought have failed to hatch
My butter changed colour
Leftovers have something running on them
My sink has fungus growing in it
Maggot stew is brewing in my garbage can
I have earwigs in my clothes, bird poop on my car
Dog shit on my shoes, somebody sneezed on my glasses
And it's only Monday

How long can one run on empty?
How many shots can I take to the chest from friendly fire?
How deep does my grave need to be
For me to feel my foot in it?

It's cold in my apartment
But the heater uses too much power
My phone, cable and internet were cut off
My car has no gas and the tires of my bike have no air.
Everything is closed

I could have found something to write home about
But I used the last paper
To write this poem that I can't live without

• • • • • • • • • • • • • • • • •

+ / -*

La meilleure façon de connaitre la fin de votre histoire
C'est de vous empressez d'en clore les chapitres

Total chaos is anarchy half of the time

I believe in injustice, it just works.

Mon dessein est de me reconnaitre
dans mes dessins de l'inconnu et du destin

The truth is unfiltered; when you doctor your words you hide a
disease on the inside

I knew there was a "lie" in what they were saying
Because in the middle of it, they were asking me to "believe"

Not seeing the power in something
Is your own weakness and only that

Come, let's make contracts with our flesh
Let's sell ourselves to each other
It's my bid for a bed in a land abounding with laundry.
I would love to press it while you're in it.
I want to make you feel weightless in my embrace
While lacing my fingers at your waist
Steal your breath away and keep you in my arms

Your voice was all the while accompanied by melodies I played
in my head, so when you left I realized where the music was

Scrivo parole che nascono da desideri e dal dolore di sapere
cercare senza avere la fortuna di potere trovare

·•·•·•·•·•·•·•·•·•·•·•·

+/-*

XX

The vision, the dream, the illusion

Au bord du rêve (Je m'endors)

Il me faut parfois ralentir
Lorsque je réalise que je peux aller plus vite

Les édifices s'inscrivent et s'effacent
De la toile blanche de l'hiver
Quelques faits divers que confère la ville où le froid vocifère
Et le message glacial est un ordre impartial
Aux corps pris dans l'alignement astral

J'entends le crépitement de lampes
Qui n'arrivent pas à rester allumées.
J'entends des enfants qu'on arrête
Chaque fois qu'ils commencent à jouer.
Je vois des couples se retenir de s'embrasser

Tous les antécédents qui mènent à tous ces précédents
Ne sont pas des accidents.
Ce qui arrive est inévitable, le reste est impossible
Mais perdus dans des palabres
On laisse l'inexorable arriver inexploré.
Mais rien ne reste, tout se transforme, à notre détriment

Prise dans les murmures d'amants dans une foule
Et les couleurs et la dance de lointaines étoiles
La vie ne connaît pas le silence.
C'est pour ça qu'elle n'est que mouvements.
Elle n'est que musique

Ce n'est peut-être que mon humanité
Mais je me vois déborder
Pour remplir les espaces laissés vides.
Je m'étire et confine une part de moi-même dans un morceau
Un banc, un paysage, une lettre, une vie

+ / -*

Mais à force de répandre mon essence
Comme pour répondre à un besoin ancestrale
Je crains ne plus être qu'une fraction de moi-même
Un mirage d'une fantaisie né dans la chaleur de ce désert
Et ma poigne sur le rebord du vide se desserre
Et je ne sais plus si je me laisse aller
Ou si ma force m'abandonne

Le résultat en reviendrait au même
Mais ce dernier me force à chercher
Le pourquoi de ce dénouement

Qu'en est-il de tout donner sans recevoir?
Et qu'en est-il de tout garder sans rien avoir?
Je perds petit à petit la notion de tout savoir et perd espoir

Je prends conscience de ma perte de connaissance
Je connais cette cadence
C'est mon cœur qui danse face à l'idée de rêver

Je connais bien ces couleurs
J'évite d'en porter
Car j'en suis le mélange étrange

Je me retrouve mieux là où je suis né
Dans ma peau, dans le noir

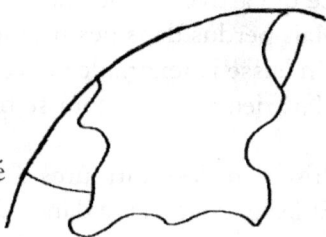

Un bruit me réveille mais je me rendors
Car il faut regarder deux fois pour croire ce que l'on voit
Lorsqu'on ne dort que d'un seul œil

+ / -*

Essence and sustenance

Changer de cap ne libère pas les captifs
De même que seuls sont prisonniers
Ceux qui cherchent la liberté

Le bond au-dessus du vide et vers l'horizon
Permet à l'inévitable de prendre place
Ce n'est qu'une préface à gagner la gloire et à perdre la face

J'attends pour voir si je vais entendre un écho
Car sinon comment saurais-je jusqu'où portent les mots.
Lorsque le monde me répond avec son silence
Devrais-je en déduire qu'il n'y a plus rien à dire?
Je réaffirme ma patience et dialogue avec ma conscience

Mon courage c'est la peur de ne pas agir
Et à chaque reprise, je me reprends, je me prends en mains
Mais maintes fois ma foi laisse place au doute
Et j'ignore d'où te viennent les impressions de ma personne
Que tu utilises pour faire pression
Mais je suis imparfait
Et présentement je cherche à corriger mes erreurs
Même si j'erre encore car je ne sais pas jusqu'où j'irai

Pendu aux aiguilles d'une montre
Je me montre impatient
Et encourage l'engrenage
D'un ton insistant
Et parfois insultant
Priant que plus tard
J'aie plus de temps
Alors que déjà j'entends
Le générique poignant
Qui précède le dénouement

J'exaspère et désespère quand je réalise que j'hallucine
Quand j'imagine à plusieurs reprises ce que j'espère.
C'est con mais quand j'y pense je compense pour le manque

Le verbe est associé à l'infini et à la création
Car la parole n'est qu'une forme du silence

De nouveau, je suis pris dans l'amertume
D'un monde qui prend fin dans ma plume
Et j'érige des mémentos pour faire place
À d'autres souvenirs oubliés aussitôt

Dessiner des endroits imaginaires
N'est fuir la réalité que quand on s'y retrouve mieux.
Ces endroits que je décris, j'en viens
Quand je m'y retrouve plus vite que dans ma rue
Ces rêves que je continue, j'y crois
Quand ils déterminent ce que j'ai en vue.
J'en fais des espoirs sur du papier
Des avions qui ne décollent que pour s'écraser
Mais ils ne prennent jamais feu
Car la flamme en mon âme ne brûle que mon cœur

Je serais magnanime quand ils comprendront
Les transformations éponymes de mon âme qui chemine
Dans le temps sans vieillir
Et dans l'espace sans mourir

Je cherche ton sourire

Je la croyais jeune et longue
Mais comme la veille
Je veille et la vielle
La nuit, se fait courte
Quand je l'y attends tout au long du jour

Je ne trouve pas le sommeil
Je sors et rentre sans voir le soleil.
Tu es ma seule source de chaleur

Je te perds pendant que tu persistes sur ton chemin

J'essaie un peu d'humour
Pour tenir l'humeur loin de la tumeur
Loin du fait que tu meurs
Et que tu ne fais que souffrir

Je veux te couper le souffle avec ce papier
Lui-même vestige d'une inspiration volée à la forêt

Je connais les recoins de ton cœur
Tous les chemins que prend ton âme
Et quand tu perdras tout de vue
Moi je saurais où tu seras

De quel métal sont tes chaînes?
Jusqu'où portent tes ailes?
Jusqu'où descends-tu avec haine?
Et quel bien fais-tu avec zèle?

Avant fous d'elle et fidèles
Ils font maintenant fi d'elle

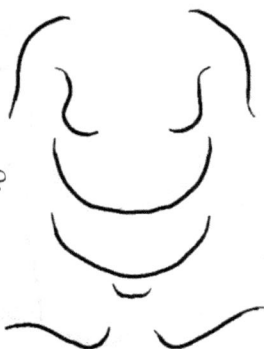

+/-*

Te souviens-tu que tu fusses elle?
Sais-tu que tu es encore belle?

Elle parle d'un ami comme d'un amant
Puis elle ne lui parle que d'amour
Mais si machin n'était pas méchant
Quelques câlins feraient le tour, avec le temps.
Mais voilà, il ne vient pas ici-bas

Ma prudence prise de court par ma pudeur
Me permit de palper sa peau et de sentir son pouls.
Son cœur y était
Battant le décompte de notre temps ensemble

Ses paroles perlent sur le pourtour de ses lèvres
Lorsqu'elle parle et son torse traduit en morse
Les mots qu'elle n'expose point
Les prières qu'elle exhausse
En cherchant son propre souffle
En proclamant sa vie

Je te parle de toi pour que tu souries
Car c'est ce que ça me fait de penser à toi

Leibsleid und liebfreud

Je ne bois pas assez pour que je me noie
Alors je prie devant une croix et m'entoure de bois.
Je ne suis nu que pour le roi des rois.
Sans maître mais à quelques mètres du sol
Je suis dans mon dernier carré
Juste sur quelques mètres carrés.
Ma foi, ma joie est au bout de mes doigts
Mais je cours juste le temps de l'effleurer
Et quand le coup de feu retentit, je suis touché

Il y avait longtemps de cela
Je cherchais l'amour là où il n'est pas.
Je sais que je lui suis transparent.
Il me passe à côté bien trop souvent
Et tous mes remèdes d'antan
Moi je les disperse tous au vent

Je n'oserais jamais sous-estimer le corps
De peur d'oublier la valeur du cœur
Mais à peine repus, je me repose.
Je rêve de jour comme je rêve de nuit
Et pour un instant, je me suffis.
Je n'arrive pas à sourire
Et quand je m'en souviens
Je recommence à souffrir.
Un tour de langue et je finis par rire
Un tour de main et je nourris mon désir

Un traitre mot me trahit sans bruit.
J'étouffe ma voix et tous mes cris
Et de nulle part je vois que tu m'écris
Sans le savoir tu me sauves la vie.
Tu as le pouvoir de me faire aimer la vie

+ / _*

Je ne sais plus comment
Danser, parler, chanter
Rire, dormir, rêver, me réveiller
Avec quelqu'un qui me plais
Encore moins quelqu'un que j'aime.
Tout m'échappe
La cadence, les paroles
L'enchantement, le sourire
Le sommeil, le lendemain

Si tu m'enlaces moi je t'embrasse.
Si tu m'empoigne moi je t'embrase.
De même que mes blessures ne se forment que pour tes soins
Bien que c'est dur tes mots doux ne viennent que de loin
Alors je reste sans réponse et sans question.
Seule ma prose reste en question.
Bien que mes rimes sont pleines de détours
Je prie de t'atteindre avant que l'on s'éteigne
Ne fut-ce qu'un jour

Mon agonie et mon euphorie viennent de la folie de cet amour

At the doors of destiny

When I opened the one door I saw countless others
Laying in alignment and a single dot of beaming light
That would enter the infinite row of rooms

It was the future in view of that one door.
I started to wonder if I didn't make a mistake.
Is this the only path that I can take?

What was beyond other doors beside this one?
What if I can't escape the future?
I already knew I can't go back
A wind was blowing at my back
Stronger and stronger
And I saw it
A film of water was preceding a wave
And every room behind me was filling

The water would soon push me into a door
Even if I don't choose one
The current would crush me
Against the thin frames
And my body would inevitably be taken in

It was time, the unstoppable force
That forces a question and demands an answer.
The answer is the present

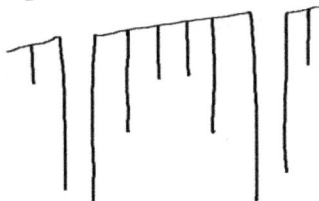

+ / -*

A pro for every con

In the absence of defense
I feel my senses heightened
In one instance, I take a chance
Choose a stance
In another, I jump the fence

On the fence on what romance is
I side with poetic justice
And from just us
I see the disturbance in my compass.
My heart beats and eats away at time
It counts what little of it remains.
In vain it spreads it through my veins
And my breath visible in the cold air
Reveals the movement the wind has to spare

I observe the stillness that fills the night.
I recall thinking it was full of demons
When it is I who's riddled with fright

I knew that at some point I would go somewhere
And somehow I would meet someone somewhat
Into the same things as me. It was something
It was something else, it was someone else

I broke the model
Because I knew I broke the mold
Doing so, I broke the code
I broke the silence

I felt a provocation from the prosecution
And pronated both feet in my stance
As I made my protracted protest at the stand

+ / -*

Though still confused, I confess the reason to my conduct
I found myself confounded by my proscription
Enabling a contest that would constitute
A conspiracy dressed as a congress
But the consecution of the execution
Had me contracting convenience
And when came the convocation
I was convinced by the conspectus in the prospectus
That my condition was a connate aspect of my provenience

Though imbued with the concept of prospect
And still lacking profit from my product
I can profess I had made progress.
I felt the conductivity in our chemistry.
My profound and profuse devotion
For a prostitute was profluent.
It was a confluent of words streaming
And converging into our common consciousness

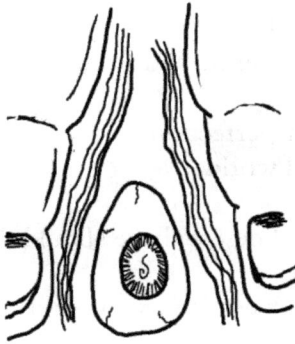

+/-*

The nines

Don't be fooled by the form
I don't fit the bill
Because I don't fit the norm

There is no greater insult
Than to be told you are not who you believe you are
And to aim lower

I chose to disregard those in disbelief

I dread the day I retire
With the frustration of remembering my best
When all the while I was trying to reach higher

I believe it's simply natural that our contributions
Should set the stage of the next step in our evolution

As dreadful as that sounds
What defines you should refine you

We're the 9s looking for perfection
In imperfect vessels and worlds

Though all the while we knew well we should do better
No such thing was done
And instead we let ourselves turn to our wild side

The disturbance became clear
As we understood how potent the distance
Could be when we deemed it unimportant in our plans

We are instances of the infinite
Attempting consistence
In every dimension and direction

+ / -*

We engulf words and gestures
Storms and oceans
Pleasure and pain
Dreams and nightmares

Like invisible black holes
We take it all in
And bend the fabric of space and time
But the tragedy lying behind the travesty
Is that we spit it all back
In a cosmic display of ineptitude

All that knowledge
All that form
We break it
And we release fumes and heat.
It all escapes us
Faster than it came in

The situation

I feel the soft shine on my skin
To be the sun on the snow.
I spin in the span of a strike
Standing on stones made of old bones
Making a slow strong stroke of ego
Grasping at what I cannot let go

Suddenly, strings, a strain on my body
Stun my thinking and I fall asleep.
On the surface, the suspense leaves me still
But on the inside, my soul swirls and spins endlessly in despair

Is it a sin to sing as soon as you give me the sign of a co-sign?
I sink deeper in sounds of the steps
Of the saint that has yet to show.
I soar with the sour taste of the scene I saw atop the sill.
Serene amidst satin I sense I am to become Satan
Singing the glory of the Lord to desire his love for only myself

Your pain hurts me

I see but a few ravens in the sky yet I can tell
There is a pattern or maybe a conspiracy.
What conspires seems seldom random

Croaking on Lili pads
You pucker frog lips in vain
And when the pain freezes your veins
You make for the city
Finally accepting love to be sexuality.
And you play make believe
And pour that Maybelline make-up on your makeup

But what do you believe is beauty?
What do you think is your duty?
Who told you what to do?
Why do you follow through?
Who did you fall for?
What pushes you over the edge?

What are you looking for?
What answer? To what question?
What do you keep for yourself?
What lies behind your defenses?

Like the unexpected seamstress
Of the fabric of reality
You hit on my door
You alter my world
You sink nails in my back
You pull at my heart
You tug at my soul

+/-*

We only break what we hold onto while in anger
We only lose what we carry around
While focusing on trivial matters
But still, we cannot let go of each other
We dare hurt and lose ourselves
Hoping we can find our path
Each time we stray from it

Lost in the silent echo of the unspoken
We can't bear to let things stay broken.
We know that what was cannot be undone
So we finish each other's lines about unfinished business

Being faithful to the faithless
Is mistaking the ones seeking power with the powerless

Be careful for I have seen you carelessly care, void of cowardice
For the ones that would hold out their hands to feed malice

It hurts to see you hand out your heart
To people who would drop it and walk all over it

You are the voice that is missing in this world
Let that resonate for a while

We only grow with resonance.
What vibrations will you share?
What waves will you dare?

Victim of poetry (No love poem today)

I have made quite a few days brighter
Humming melodies of sorrowful songs

I don't replay songs, re-watch movies, re-read books
I replay the feeling of letting something else in
I remember one of my many births

I'm aiming for a flow, a carefully curated stream of citations
Quotes of poets, notes on the practice of noticing
A lotus in mud and blood and if it's enticing that'd be the icing

I only feed on select bites with the aftertaste of thirst
Then satiate my desire with drops of hunger for more

I only seek words above the silence, above pretense
I give my imagination free reign
Attempting to build myself a kingdom

I need texts that will withstand the test of time
Testaments that can be the new commandments

I forgive things done half-heartedly
For there are still those with only half of themselves
But it increases my craving for the carving of creation
By hacking away at materials
Such as wood, ice, rock and paper

All of them can only be hit once in the same spot.
In essence, all one does is find an image
Already drawn on the inside
And shed everything else to the ground.

Like carving a sculpture out of a tree trunk
I call a poem out to the surface of a page

+ / _*

I find serendipity in propinquity.
I let new encounters and each new scenery
Provide me with a recipe to write poetry

I gain one life each time I feel alive.
I make it work because I must make it count

I collect my thoughts
And filter them with the intention of an emotion.
All the while in denial
I don't try to get rid of my addiction

A poem to me is simply a couple of lines I will read many times
And my curse will have me rehearsing
Verses onto concourses until I lay in a hearse

It may be a detour but
I will explore humanity
Before I aim for the divine

Even when I forget to write words that I believe to be true
I wait for them to come back and they do
Because they are things that travel with me
They are things I never leave behind

Practice aloud a lie among those who know the truth
And you will know the gravity
Of murmuring the truth among those who believe the lie

What cannot be articulated cannot be used to lie
So if I cannot say what I feel, I don't try.
Be it poetry or prose, I am at the mercy of my muse's ruse
And she is only amused when she hears music
And if she so chooses things end on a sad note

I can't write you a love poem today

Steam

Le papier contient d'innombrables mondes
Jusqu'à ce que je mette l'emphase
Sur l'un d'eux avec quelques phrases

Ce passe-temps prend beaucoup de mon temps
Alors quand la pub joue, je baisse le son
Je passe à autre chose, alors elle revient de plus en plus
Car je regarde de moins en moins
Bien que c'est en vain
Car je les connais déjà
Depuis plus de vingt ans.
Je sais ce qu'ils vendent. Je sais ce qui me manque.
Je le chercherai, quand je ne pourrais plus m'en passer.
Je l'achèterai, quand le prix sera plus élevé.

Je ne déguste que de ce qui me régale
Le reste m'est bien égal

Je n'ai plus le temps de voir le temps qu'il fait
Je perds mon temps ailleurs.
S'il fait beau tant mieux sinon tant pis.
Ce qui compte c'est la chaleur dans mon cœur
Et l'âge de mon âme

Maudis soient ces mots-dièse, l'hypertexte et l'arobase.
Mon malaise ne met pas fin à mes mots
Mais mes maux finissent par infiltrer mes mots.
J'écris sans filtre même si ce n'est pas sans fautes
Et mes doigts en apprennent à prendre la fuite
Pour revenir au début sans faute

Je me retrouve désabonné
Des rituels annuels
Des révérences et des ritournelles

+ / -*

De la tendance et de l'attention qu'elle requière
Des nouveaux bidules et des nouvelles
Des bolides qui se ressemblent
Et qu'il semble que tout le monde assemble
Et des facsimiles qu'ils assimilent

Mais j'assume et présume
Que sur ces quelques milles
Il y a plus d'espèces que ces mules
Malgré tout l'espace qu'ils consument

Mais ces mâles s'enfoncent jusqu'au cou
En mettant les doigts dans le mauvais trou
Et ce n'est pas que je plains les trous du cul
Mais je les comprends peu
Pour ne point dire pas
Et ils parlent beaucoup
De comment ils arrivent au combien
De leurs prouesses et aux largesses
Qu'ils professent avec allégresse
En remuant la graisse de leur fesses

Et ces femmes, elles me saoulent
Si je ne leur bouche pas la bouche
En leur roulant une pelle.
Elles me rappellent que mon nom s'épelle
Avec les lettres de la solitude
Et elles me content tant bien comment elles y arrivent
Aux océans du bonheur et aux épaves à la dérive
Et à la paresse qui accompagne le fait d'être une compagne
Alors qu'elles se brisent le dos
En couchant avec des hommes qui ne font pas le poids

Et c'est pour ça que tous deux
Les sexes et les genres n'ont pas de peau
•–•–•–•–•–•–•–•–•–•–•–•–•

+ / -*

Were there no continuity to time, we would create it
Starving for a future and a long line of shots at second chances

The future shall once again become the past.
The present is but the furnace where time is consumed.
The past and the future simply linger as memories and dreams.

Onto heretofore unknown paths
Hitting a wall while going forward
Only means you are going the right way.
Nothing worth moving on is an easy journey

I too want to trust that the universe is not expanding
But rather that the stars send us their light as guides
So that, one day, we too may join the final step
To this life and onto the next

With these finite lives, let's live forever

Tell me your deepest thoughts until we figure out telepathy

If you think of love as a knife, it will cut you
Beware of the blade in your mind

What else can we say to each other?
The same way I must lie to you, if you make it clear you want
me to, I must also find someone who will have the truth

Je ne garde en mémoire qu'un petit nombre de personnes
Bientôt je ne saurais plus comment te trouver.
Tu seras l'une de ces notes de bas de page.
Je te trouverai flottant sur l'eau quand je ferai naufrage
Quand une larme de trop me rappellera de toi

· ● · ● · ● · ● · ● · ● · ● · ● · ● · ● · ●·

XXI

The symbols, the symmetry, the symphony

+ / -*

Peace of mind

Hell is the Heaven we deny ourselves

Flip if you must.
If your rage comes
From what I put on this page
Flip if you must

Could you appreciate the irony
Of being a writer and a waiter
If all you were asked to do was to wait
And all you could do was to write?

They tell you to stay in line
But there is no help for those waiting

I am tired of dialogues of demagogues
Self-masturbating into demi-gods
And flattery over mouth flatulence
For fat cats in flat lands

I am troubled because the system works
And I am setting out to try new things

I feel there is a distance in each memory.
The horizon is full of unattainable possessions.
My reach stretches with my mind until I flatline
And lay flat for what's on the line

There are times I get stuck with all the answers in my head
Because aside the question you ask me
I hear loudly all the ones you don't
So I ponder on the question of honesty

+ / -*

Could it be easier if we were honest to each other
Or would you then tell me there is no hope for a brother?

Would you buy it, if I sold myself better?
Or would you follow my own advice about advertisement
For I believe you need less the more they sell?

The thing is my handling of things got out of hand
When I felt out of touch and fell out of grace

Drop a marble and follow it
Until it stops rolling.
I was there
At the lowest place in the room

Optimistically leaving some things up to the mystic
I moved away from the incoming rolling fog
To enter a subtle mist
But I remember drowning
And I remember the snow in the ocean
And making peace with the wither of my winter
That would follow me forever

Soon looking at the moon
On the surface of the water
A long glance would help me find
In Poseidon a liking to Hypnos

After hitting rock bottom, softly I woke up
To a fix and a pick me up

I am a neophyte to cryptobiosis
So bear with me as I go through metamorphosis

I took my new mind out for a spin
Like breaking a horse through the valley

+ / _*

To be frank I don't fear to be flanked
Because of the people at my side.
I will not lose heart or ground
Even if I get lost, I will be sound

I am not stargazing
I am counting my lucky stars
Counting the ones still shining
And if those flames are the past, I am reminiscing
All the worlds I used to live in that are now missing

If you accept that there are things you don't know
Then you will have an answer for every question

This is the prognosis
From an apprentice
Of a dangerous praxis

We are but men of minutes in the last hour
Hanging on promises of futures with libation
Feasting on presents from past pursuits of satiation.
Nonetheless let me extend this invitation:

Welcome to the shining night
Where we moonlight shining in the darkness
Humming with heart a harmony we can harness

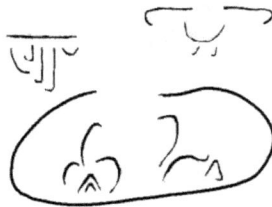

Seul meurent ceux dans le silence

Ils étaient des femmes et des hommes confus
Fondant en larmes confondues
Avec des cœurs qui ne battent plus
Dans des corps battus
Et convaincu de ce que j'ai vu
D'où je suis venu
J'allais en faire part aux parvenus
Quand je me suis souvenu
M'être longtemps retenu
De devenir un détenu
Et comme leurs oranges tenues
Me dérangent et que je préfère être nu.
Mais ma peur n'a pas cru
Comme mon indignation qui à l'insu
M'a porté à me préparer à être vaincu
Tant que je révèlerai la forme de l'incongru
Qui reste encore inconnue
Car avec le temps elle a muée et m'a mu
Et je mourrai ayant fait tout ce que je pu.
Que l'on marche dans les rues
Que l'on touche ceux qu'ils tuent
Que reprennent vie ceux qui l'avaient perdue de vue
Car s'éclaircit tout ciel quand il a plu

Un mot avant que mon cœur ne brise

Un seul mot de plus et c'était fait
J'entendais mon cœur briser

Mais que venais-je donc chercher?
Je savais déjà où j'allais
Mais la tête dans les plis d'une carte
Je me perdais à imaginer des fins de routes inexplorées
Mais, loin de là, je n'y mettrais jamais les pieds.
J'avais encore les choses en main
Saurais-je quoi en faire demain?
Ai-je atteins aujourd'hui mes limites?
Je compte les jours et marque les dates
Mais je doute de ce qui m'attend et rien ne m'y apprête.
Ce que je sais, c'est que j'en suis là

Un mot de plus et c'est fait
J'entends déjà mon cœur briser

Mon temps est compté
Un seul traitre mot après ton long silence
Et je passerai le reste de ma vie à recoller les morceaux
Sans me rappeler de ce que j'avais
Sans savoir ce que je fais

Je ne sais pas si cette accalmie est le paradis.
L'as-tu déjà dit? L'enfer, est-ce donc ceci?
Je me repli et me remplit de mots qui m'étouffent
De peur d'y mettre un autre qui me tuera

Extra

You know...
I could stay
Maybe listen, maybe answer, maybe ask
Sometimes smile
Others, touch.
I could leave
And... come back
We could go eat
Out, or here
Or your place or mine

We could go dance
Watch a movie or check out some live painting
Listen to poetry, look at sculptures, watch a play
Or go to a zoo, a museum, a circus, a fair, a park, a beach...

We could do it, do it all, all the way
The very stretch of all your imagination
The very edge of all your fears
In and out of all the boxes
You fear to be in
The ones they try to put you in
We could live together
We could live forever

But all of that is going to cost you extra

I don't like dancing without you

I lost sight of a quarter of your lips
In the blink of an eye
A quick and subtle eclipse
From the rotation of your hips.
You had lost perception of depth
So you didn't know how close I was.
I had come to you so fast
But your hand was taken already
And the crowd closed on you
Like a sea closing a path where it was parted

That was the last time I saw you.
Now I know not to close my eyes
Too much is lost with the distance.
I also lost the will to dance
Because I lost sight of my chance
But my body keeps changing its stance
So I can tell why you think I enjoy this.
I understand why you would think I like this
But I don't, not without you

+/-*

Requiem with tritones for maximae vulvae

There is sin for those without a hell or a heaven
Those asking for more colours out of sunsets in the horizon
Telling long stories because they fear
Each moment to be misunderstood
Scared of analysis paralysis
In the face of a cornucopia of minutia

The hardest things are the easiest
When that's all that remains to be done
Which helps to further the story
Of breakthroughs and the eventual wall and downfall

The tritone sets a rather fitting red undertone
To the chanting on the prowess
Of the powerful paraphernalia called pussies.
The strongest to hold true to this manifest
Simply rebelled against love; the form and the function

In a world where chemical imbalance
Would bind you to a single person
Freedom was to find balance
On the tips and mouths of the many
Like birds only pausing to regain the sky
Unable to simply jump and stay there

Ironically those more grounded would think they found heaven
And it is on those trees that they would build nests
High as can be, where a fall would be deadly
And in the uncanny and strong winds
That would blow through the forest, many would fall
And those who did
After forgetting they could fly
Never flew again

+ / -*

Like bears they might at times rock the trunks
And do onto others what was done onto them.
A vengeance protracted into a vindication
If one can prove herself vicarious

To some, love is a terrible order
Where imagination dies inside infatuation.
You begin to see your future as it simplifies
Into a straight path to your demise.
A frightful vision that you accept
As though you had gone through an epiphany

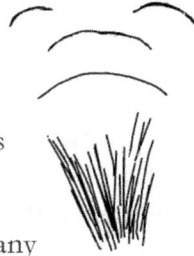

Though seen as maniacs many nymphs would practice
And learn to preach the contradictions of love
Where a simple invitation becomes confusing
Because though we know the destination
We don't see how to get there

The origin of this trouble, we put ourselves in, is surely a sin.
When one accounts for all the hurt, surely, love must be a sin
A malpractice of inconsiderate people

The branches of a tree stretch
And carry the leaves in the sunlight
And in winter or when the trees wither
You can see how much of a fight survival took

This truth hidden, behind clothes
On ephemeral sunny and warm days
Would make the nymphs vulnerable when divested.
Though it was their charm
There was this awkward recurring moment
Where the bare essentials could be inefficient or insufficient
And the worse was when deviants would dig in
Even as they derived out loud how they felt deprived
When really they were just proving to be depraved

+ / -*

Though inelegantly laid
A trap will more than a few times catch prey
So there, amid laundry would lie all those bodies
Truly bodies and beds of lies

The vividity of the trivial makes for confusion.
While they try to sort things out
In a puzzle of pieces made of people
Grabbed or rather scooped out of the masses
Like randomly picking flowers and gardeners
To concoct a perfume that would linger
Something to hide the waning and the withering
Making a mask to hide the passage of time
Conflicted with the desire to move on
And the acknowledgment of the resistance against such drive
The nymphs are afflicted
With the affection for colours and scents
That would create this illusion of forever
No matter how many times things would be over

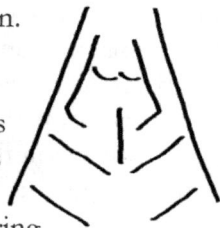

No mind is spotless
So there must be an obstruction to the eternal light.
Slipping into the salience of their silence
They find solace in knowing
They are committing themselves to committing a crime

They were serious about chaining themselves to their deviance
While dancing in a chain of daisies

Battle at the banks

Though in denial
Thinking this could bring peace
They increase their pace
Singing their country and customs
So they would fall in and fall as one

As rile with guile
And fill with words
Mouths stained with bile
The Nile, too, fills
With those who never lived on its banks

But the banks count
On all those shells shelling out death
Out of tanks
Breaking ranks
Of dead men walking
Knowing on the inside
That the outside has come
Like a poison
And it has taken root within

And from under their skin
They see the fiery greeting
Of metal traversing them
As they transcend
Into heroes and martyrs of war

+ / -*

Mezcla de islas

En el calor de la luz de la mañana
Somos solo una mezcla de islas móviles
Esperando por la atracción de la luna
Para acortar la distancia entre nuestras almas

Why do we have each other?

My mother had me
I came into this world
Soaked with her blood
Hers and my father's in my veins

And a brother of my father
Made his blood spill

I have sisters and I have her, my mother.
We've had each other.
There were others
There are more of us
All the time
And you could feel
You have them
But you lose them
And then you wonder

You wonder as you wander.
What was all that about
Having each other
And losing one another
Losing sight of each other?

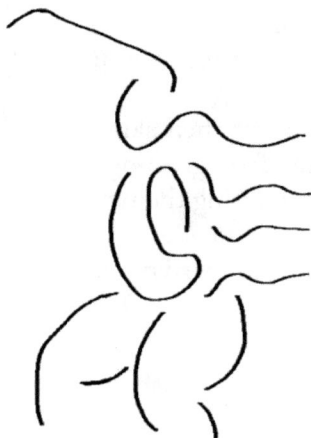

Dark Ascension

I used to err on my errands
I never believed in straight paths
I wandered without being lost
I corrected my errors at a cost
I strayed from my bearing
My eyes saw sights I was not meant to know
I questioned often if I was dreaming
I tried to imagine what it feels like to be awake
I wanted to know what was at stake

The greatest the fear to die
The most one feels alive.
So I gambled my life away with a die
Never knowing neither when nor where I would arrive

I have the feeling that my foot is on the break
I have limitations I am not meant to have
There must be another level
I am sure of it now, I know why
I am trying to ascend
Cutting through the sky
In a fight to the bitter end.
I do not go lightly into paradise
I cannot avert my eyes
I have pictured the shape of my prize
I can tell the sweet bullshit in their lies

+ / -*

Lawd

First it was one lap
She sat on my lap
And I heard a band snap
Then she asked for a slap.
Her wiggling had me hardening
I knew it was a trap
I knew it would keep me going.
She fit the bill as the bill got thicker
She sped up and spun quicker
She held tight and held me close
Wringing me into believing her lies as she goes.
Her voice was bullshit sweet with romance.
She bit her lips and licked them
While panting, panties still at her ankles
Locked on her heels, her real love handles.
I know she faked some of those eruptions
I went to her because of her fountain
I wanted to drench my body in youth

I can tell as she drives me in deeper.
I know when she comes.
I keep going and work the tip
As she works for the tip.
We make a mess then go on a while longer.
I tell myself I got her good
But she comes and sets the mood
Bittersweet until the very end.
I am hellbound, but she'll stick it in and stick around
And go one more round
Until I run out of money to spend

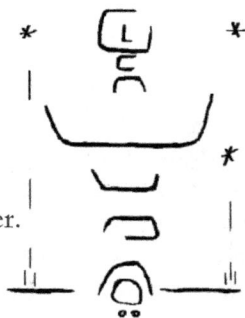

+ / -*

L'arnacœuse

Elle joue avec le feu
Plusieurs flammes à la fois.
Sans réserves pour son foie
Elle prend de tout
Et quand tout lui revient, elle a la foi
Les paumes jointes et les joues peintes
Par le maquillage qui coule encore
Sur des marques indélébiles sur son corps
Des mots qui ne la quittent pas
Qu'elle porte fièrement
Car elle ne sait pas comment s'en défaire.
On ne lui a appris que comment s'y faire.
Cet ange à peine déchu que l'on nomme déjà Lucifer
Chantait il n'y a pas si longtemps les louanges des cieux
Mais les pieds sur terre, peu restent pieux.
Sous ses vêtements courts et serrés son cœur se resserre
Pris dans la torsion du tourment qui la fait tourner en bourrique

Elle fait couler une fausse joie dans ses veines.
Elle tombe, en deçà, plus bas que son statut de reine.
Avec des petites morts au bout des lèvres
Elle baise Azraël et l'embrasse en une transe
Que l'on croirait être sa seule façon de vivre

Royal and raw

I'm fucked; royally.
Yes, it's the queen that fucks me
The one on that pretty penny
The one who sent governors
To ascend laws that cripple this country
The one on the money, the one sitting on our gold
The one waving behind that bulletproof glass
With gloves on because she thinks the air has crass.
I can feel her figure embossed on the metal
I can tell it's her with my hands grasping at straws.
I remember her worth, her size and her flaws
To me she is just a number, a small one
That repeats and that beats me into working
Then she takes me out back and fucks me.
She makes me realize I'm worthless
No matter how much I get
No matter how long I keep her with me

I keep our first president in my wallet too
When I bend them together in that tight space
I hope he knows what to do

A sculptor and a captor

He took a chisel and chipped away at the ebony
Until they made a child
Yes he dug into her body
He reached as deep as her womb could stretch
He heaved for as long as she could moan
He cut her deep
He salted her wounds with her tears
He shook her while keeping her still
He did as beasts would in their last hour
He turned her into a crime scene
He turned her and gave her some green
He left her with grief with a grin
He had stolen her footing after hitting her chin
He had never heard of fine china
He had never held porcelain
He had never cared for a single thing in the world
But today he comes to see his son
He talks of seeing the light
He talks to her as if it made it right
As if he never knew of the sun
For he is all the darkness of night
He is the darkness of that night
The night she recalls at every visit
The night where she wants to hurt him
The night she cannot sleep
The night they made that boy
That she prays will be a real man
The night she became a woman
The night she became a mother

Letters to break your heart

There is a letter out there
That has all the words it takes to break your heart
A few words that when carried by the wind
Could take your breath and your life away
A few suggestions, a few orders with weight

There are words made of gunpowder.
There are sentences written for freedom.
They are but just words, but they are not justice.
There is a way to say you will live while all others die.
There is a path made of landmines.
There are houses made of mortar.
There are rivers naturally flowing with poison.
It's all there in the acts of war
In the proliferation of freedom
In the transmigration of fear
In letters made of words uttered in silence

There are words that would make you lose faith.
There are images that would blind you with the color red.
There are spaces in between those things
Interludes in the shape of turning pages
Intermissions with the roar of meaningless chatter

There is a silence that will have you sleep soundly
While the sleeping stops for many others
Eyes wide open as they wake constantly to their last moment
Caught in the unbelievable story that their dream stopped

There is a silence made of words
Buried inside paper and between satellites
That will have you believe words are the greatest weapons yet.
There are words I could cut your eyes with
But I need you to go on to read even more

+ / -*

I want you to muster the strength to bleed out
From seared wounds on the flesh of others.
I want you to master the art of taking in all that is abhorring.
I want you to be disgusted
So disgusted you will change the world.
I want you to be so hurt
You will love again
You will love everyone
You will love yourself

Do you fight to keep the freedom
Of people justice would put away?
Would you fight, truly, for freedom?

I will be sick tomorrow

The moment we say goodbye
The door, the stairs, the elevator...
They all become the new hangout
The after party, the place to be
And all the things we were leaving for later
We're dealing with now
At ungodly hours
With unrested bodies.
We already know we need to sleep on this
But we cannot seem to close our eyes
Not so soon, not while we have each other
So we talk for an hour
In the hallway, the parking lot, the car
And somehow we spend more time there
Than at that table we always get
Or on the comfortable couches in your living room.
We must have a thing for endings
We keep it all in since the beginning
We do it, again and again
We take all the time we need
Especially when we knew
We didn't get as much as we wanted
But now I'll be late to work tomorrow
I'll be calling sick

+ / -*

You first

The way you recite those words
Twirling your fingers
Rolling your tongue
Swaying your hips
I cannot help but to want to make love to you
Yet I wait for you to finish
I wait for you to come
First
And I realise you were making love to me
You had those fingers running on me
You rolled that tongue in me.
You made foreplay out of wordplay.
Soon my forte with swordplay would be on display
But you go first.
I want you to speak first
Because I love the way you do it
It is known to many as taboo
But that trance, that stance, that voodoo
It is love permeating the air
And the heat is turned up.
I can hardly keep my clothes on.
Actually, I am already divested
Because you touch me
In the deepest parts of my soul
With a few words

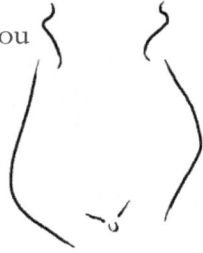

You are my rock
And with one stone
You struck two birds

+/_*

Je ne ravale jamais mes mots
Ils descendent comme des poings
Surtout quand j'en fais un

Je t'envoie quelques missives aussi lourdes que des ogives
Et bien que je vise ton cœur je ne cherche pas à te blesser

I need a robot; you cannot turn off women.
Although that last phrase probably did.

Indefinitely, I hesitate as builds the shape of the infinite
Pulling the first stroke further outside the boundaries of my
canvas

I just want the elitist on the illicit. Just the illest shit.
Just to illustrate what's a mind on another state

No one has the might to reverse the flow of a river
But countless times, a drop will find itself at the top
No one has the power to reverse the flow of time
But countless times, a soul will relive the same moments

When you laugh at the thoughts
Crossing your mind as light dressed in twinkles comes back
From bursting stars at the edges of space
In a cloud of materials for our vessels
Your eyes betray you. They tell me you are not here

Avant je croyais que mon prochain c'était la personne à côté de
moi. Je sais maintenant que c'est celle qui suit

Si l'erreur est humaine, est-ce une erreur d'être humain?

•·•·•·•·•·•·•·•·•·•·•·•·•·•·•·•·

+ / -*

XXII

Sentience

Parce qu'on vient de loin

On doit laisser transparaitre qu'on n'est pas d'ici
On doit les laisser savoir qu'on a plus de savoir
Que les quelques notions
Qu'ils nous rationnent sous forme d'éducation
On doit leur faire comprendre que même le chez nous
Au milieu de nulle part c'est partout ailleurs
On doit leur montrer que nous ne faisons qu'arriver
Que nous ne faisons que commencer
Et pourtant, déjà on excelle là où plusieurs faillissent.
Malgré tout, on se lève pendant que tant tombent.
Après tout, on laisse une empreinte indélébile

Chaque premier pas que nous faisons est le millième

Si nos pères se lèvent tôt et rentrent tard du boulot
C'est parce qu'ils peuvent en faire part sans en dire un mot
Et si nos mères sourient encore à l'ajout d'un autre fardeau
C'est parce qu'elles n'ont pas peur
De porter le monde sur leur dos.
Elles ont porté nos sœurs et nos frères
Qui parfois en font trop
De peur de ne pas en faire assez
Car l'exemple à suivre nous impose
D'être nous aussi exemplaires
Car nous ne pouvons pas être exemptés dans ces terres volées
Car chaque pas que nous faisons de l'avant
Commence en Afrique

+ / -*

Tu me pardonneras

Malgré le respect que j'ai pour les femmes
L'amour que je ressens pour nos mères
Les prières que je répète pour nos sœurs
Mon corps est comme celui de mes frères
Pris dans le tourment au tournant de tes courbes.
Dans l'écho de tes paroles, il fait bien trop chaud pour la raison
En faire usage serait surement hors saison.
Je te dénudais quand tu articulais tes idées
Je t'écoutais. Je te jure que j'écoutais
Mais cela n'a fait que renforcer mon érection
Cela n'a fait que nourrir ma déviante passion.
Je me voyais séparer tes lèvres
Je me prévoyais dans tes bras
Alors que nous serions pris comme des rats
À la fois à l'aise et surpris, fiers et dans l'embarras.
Je ne te mentirais pas
Je déchirais la nuit avec mes hurlements
Je délirais dans l'attente.
J'imaginais les goûts de ta peau, de ta sueur et de tes larmes
J'entendais déjà tes gémissements, tes cris et tes eaux
Remplir les espaces encore libres
Entre les fréquences de la nuit
Les chocs de nos cuisses
Et la frénésie lourde dans nos souffles
Pendant qu'on se soufflerait des mots doux
Dans un lit qui tient dur.
Je concoctais à chaque fois un plan qui tombait à plat.
Je cherchais les mots qui uniraient nos corps comme nos esprits.
Tu me pardonneras
Je t'écoutais. Je te jure que j'écoutais
Mais mon corps me disait que je devais te toucher
Et je ne sais pas jusqu'où ni jusque quand.
Je te mentirais si je disais que je suis sérieux
Mais je suis épris d'une façon souvent méprise pour de la luxure

Mais si je peux me permettre le luxe de te connaitre
Je serais le plus riche des hommes.
Je ne sais pas si je te souille
Et avec le temps je sens que je rouille
Mais je me sens incapable de dérailler.
Je suis sur une voie que je ne peux pas quitter.
J'entends ta voix et je me sens m'élever
Et le canon entre tes lèvres, je me vois déjà tirer.
Tu me pardonneras

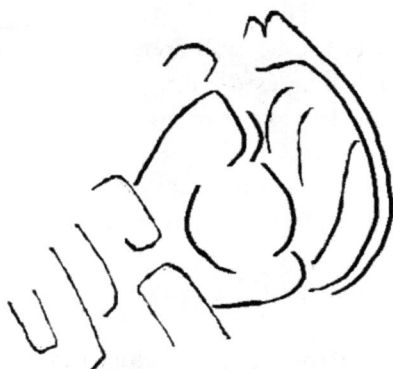

Memo derrière ma prochaine toile

L'histoire derrière cette toile nue
C'est le récit d'une civilisation disparue.
C'est le compte d'un rêve révolu
Les réserves d'un ex-détenu.
Ce n'est pas simplement l'image de la pureté
Ni le résultat d'une paresse sans pareil.
C'est le mélange de toutes les couleurs qui y réfléchissent.
C'est la franchise d'un morceau noir sous la lumière.
C'est la somme de mille poils d'un pinceau qui fléchissent
Entre les doigts secs d'un peintre sans muse ni muselière.
Une toile vide c'est l'arrière-plan flou
D'un complot incomplet
Concocté par des observateurs fous.
C'est la vérité décrite sans supposition.
C'est la honte de trouver de la pudeur pour toutes les positions.
C'est une insulte insolite
À toute honorable personne qui peut être offensée.
C'est la défense contre les mauvais dires
Et la traitrise envers le sens de l'insensé

Why the poor never waged war

The poor never wanted to wage war.
They know it doesn't solve a thing.
They know it would make a poor soul sadly richer.
So those not drafted or forced into human shields
Those that survived and don't know
What good hatred could do for them
They press onward, whatever the direction.
But they seem to always know their destination.
Their everyday lives were never quiet
And still they would make for the city.
They would circle the hill
They would walk down to the nearest road
A pathway of sand, torn plastic and strips of newspaper.
They would walk hours for water.
They would run to school, they would make do with little.
They would do great things and stay humble.
They would keep a smile and be courteous.
They knew something about happiness.
They understood a few secrets about life
So they carried on not wondering about what was coming.
They had all seen death in the eye
But there were times they would pause
Somewhere behind a tree unseen maybe by anyone
Or in a mourning crowd around a coffin
A street corner, a highway exit, a house
And though they knew about all the happiness
And beauty left in this world
Still they mixed silence with sobs
And poured libations from their eyes
Made of spirits that matured for millennia.
They knew something we all forgot
And there will be a tear to your eye
When you remember and see all the hurt that was done
And the love we owe each other

+ / -*

Cosa è l'amore

Per me, fa sempre buio
Allora sogno
Della luce
Nel tuo sorriso dolce
Di quando saremo insieme

Se prima non viene la primavera
Forse verrai come prima
Nel freddo de la sera

Sarò l'uomo che amavi
Nel passato in cui ti ricordi
Solo quando cadono calde lacrime
Sulla tua pelle
Senza che sappi perché
Senza che sappi per te
Cosa è l'amore

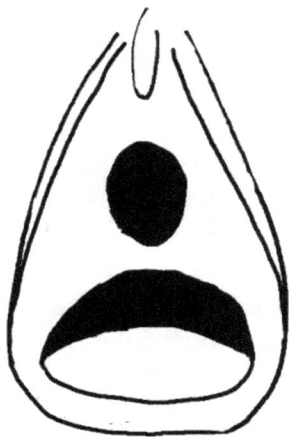

+ / -*

Not much but love and pains as such

Drawn like cosmograms against the night
We silently sigh
As the next constellation shines
In the shape of a signature after the verb

On our little rock
We remain attached to the bulwark
Of a shipwreck that became a water-break
For streams bent on having the land awash
In the blue of the sky

We stumble, still proud of being the architects of the dark
Humbly risking aberrated steps
And shapeless erections
In the unseen of the abyss
And the noise of a grim joke
Lined with the punch in it

And as though drinking
At the fountain of youth
We feed the force in our fists
As we prepare to knock on each other's defenses
While we make ourselves defenseless
While we remember the sensation of getting knocked senseless

Though favouring the attack
We acknowledge the incoming failures
And the few already falling

In the roar of the herbs
The height of things is reached
Through flight

+ / -*

We are running
From those three lights
And sleepless nights
From the dread of day
And the toil of tomorrow
Running into a still
Running still

But in that running
We end up chasing what we love
And treat it as such
And when we get it all
We find a way to hold onto it
Even if to some, even if later
It might not look like much

À la fermeture (Ouverts l'un à l'autre)

On se rapprochait du regard
On s'y retrouvait
Dans cet entre-deux fait par nos yeux
Et la distance se raccourcissait au milieu
À une vitesse où le temps ne s'écoule pas

Je ne l'entends que la deuxième fois
Le serveur dit qu'ils sont déjà fermés
C'est pour ça qu'ils ont commencé à nettoyer
C'est pour ça qu'ils nous ont fait payer
Une addition pour quelques petites portions
Faits avec amour, faute de potions

On n'avait pas vu le temps passer

Je fis retomber mon regard que l'on avait dévié
Et sur ton visage je vu la dernière question
Que tu poserais à cette table, après tant d'autres

Tu la poses entre tes mains.
Tu la retiens à peine entre tes doigts
Mais, enfin, tu laisses filler l'interrogative définitive

Tu savais que je la connaissais.
Je la prévoyais, je l'ai écrite sur tes lèvres.

Nous l'avions conçue avec les mouvements subtils de nos yeux
Qui oscillaient alors qu'on ne voyait que devant
Et de nos pieds pris dans l'étroit souterrain fais de bois

Nous savions que le temps passe
Nous l'avions ignoré, nous l'avions mis de côté
Nous ne voulions que de la distance que l'on avait raccourcie

+ / -*

On s'était posé tant de questions
Que nous avons fini par comprendre
Que nous savions où tout cela irait

Oui tu connaissais la réponse
Mais je te l'ai donné pour te faire plaisir
Je venais d'apprendre que ça me ravissait de te faire sourire

Bands rain

He looked at his hand
He had diamonds in spades
He could get a few hearts
But chose to hit gentlemen's clubs

He had learned the power of the dollar
That power that makes paper into a collar
Crooked witchcraft and wretched wizardry
That would let him cast a spell on the glittery

A hex made out of hundreds
That would have a girl
Dance under the influence
Of falling bills

The strongest substance

Now a few tricks gawk and gasp
Their gaze stuck on what a dime
Dropping for dollars, would change into
Suits of birth day, suits of innocence
Both perverted in fumes of subtle incense

Crime par excellence (Arme maîtresse, Le monde ne suffit pas)

Pour la toile
Chaque coup de pinceau
Est une tache indélébile
Même quand elle se retrouve sous une autre
Parmi deux couches
Chaque trait, chaque courbe est une blessure

Les toiles blanches ne sont pas de la bonne couleur
Disent les peintres
Les feuilles vierges ne connaissent rien du monde
Disent les écrivains
L'argile doit cuir pour avoir de la valeur disent les potiers
La roche et le bois sont trop gras disent les sculpteurs

Le monde ne suffit pas disent les artistes

Des coups de marteaux
Des coups de pinceaux
Des coups de haches
Des coups de génie
Voilà la forme du désordre
Qu'ils mettent un peu partout
Pour décrire la beauté
Qui les entoure déjà

L'art est notre défaut.
C'est notre incapacité
De partager notre point de vue.
C'est notre désir de refaire le monde

Nous ne savons toujours pas
Comment présenter une rose au monde entier
Sans l'arracher du sol

Sans la couper à la tige
Sans couper des arbres
Sans inonder des plaines
Sans raser des forêts
Sans miner le sol
Sans creuser dans des montagnes
Sans chauffer la planète
Sans tuer d'autres espèces
Sans nous entre-tuer

L'art, c'est notre arme maîtresse.
C'est le crime par excellence.
C'est le péché né de notre faiblesse
Qui se répète grâce à l'ignorance

+/-*

In the skin of eternal summer (Nirvana para Hijos del sol, I would make a star)

Because we live
What we do becomes alive
We bring about these creatures
That are made up of forces
That take the shape of god to some
And that of the devil to others

The good we spread becomes our hope
And it will watch over our fates
So long as we nurture it
And the evil we unleash and let roam
Will keep on feasting on our kind
Until we put it down

I am honing my senses and my skills
Boiling on the inside with a raging fire
Just to shine in my last moments

What will kill me is the only thing I cannot survive
Everything else, I do not fear, I don't think about it.
So I am preparing myself to meet my limits
Because I have to make the best of my defeat.
I have to lose it all in the best way I know
And I have to learn better ways still.
I am learning to die
In every meditation
In every movement

So I find myself daydreaming at night
Keeping strange hours
Trying to take my time
And make the most of it before it's up

+ /-*

Though I was at times shunned
For falling following my way home
I tried being a bright son
And where it was darkest, I shined:
In my own shadow
In my own skin

And then it came to me.
If I was wearing the kiss of a star
I should just leave one behind

If there was a mark I would like to leave it would be a star
A dimming light in the middle of emptiness and darkness
That would be seen for centuries after it dies

Insight in hindsight

With my ebbing breath in a storm that can't abate
Like a moth to a flame I take the bait
Of a dour demon that looms over any attempt at happiness
While I take shots to the head for things I took to heart

Juices that made this ambrosia more potent
Catch me in the context of a complex
But still stupid and intrepid
I sip off this tepid liquid in a cup from cupid

Though frustrating, it's inspiring
To remember that I forgot one more thing
I could have said or done
To get another smile out of you
Surely, next time

I find a piece of happiness
In your hands talking their way into mine
Through the translation of our longing in a language
Etched onto our radiant bodies
With words only known to the mute

Prickly spots abounding with moisture
Sudden shudders and slow embraces
Make us undress each other
As if to pare off the layers we cannot consume

The insight of lovers blind to all others
Can be seen in the delicate touch
Of wandering on one another
With an itchy finger
Planting the seed of laughter
To steal a smile and a kiss
All in the recipe of making forever

La crainte du connu

Si j'articule une idée
Sous forme d'une graine
Dans les recoins de ton esprit
Là où reposent les moments que nous avons partagé
Y laisseras-tu le temps passer au printemps?

L'ironie du temps qui passe
C'est qu'on devrait le passer
En créant des moments inoubliables
Où l'on voudrait qu'il s'arrête

Un orchestre accompagnait tous tes pas et toutes tes humeurs
Et parfois il te trahissait en révélant le secret de ta douleur
Mais ces fois-là, ton corps aussi n'était pas de ton côté
Et ça t'enrageais de te savoir si simple à déchiffrer
Car nombreux étaient les tours qu'on t'a fait.
Tous tes mouvements devenaient musique
Et j'en fredonnais les mélodies en pensant à toi

Quand tu te sentais menottée à la monotonie
Un crescendo emplissait la salle
Avec une assourdissante cacophonie

Je n'ose pas poser mon regard sur tes lèvres
Car pendant que j'y pends
Je me vois déjà t'approcher
Pour te voler un baiser.
Mais que fais-tu de mes charmes
Toi qui me désarme

Le secret de nos moments de silence
C'est que l'on reste à l'écoute
Et on apprend, sans doute
À reconnaitre les mots

Qui n'y changent rien.
On s'établie un système de valeur
Car même les vauriens cherchent le bonheur

Ces petits moments
Qui n'appartiennent qu'à nous
Survivent dans les endroits
Et les présents que nous nous sommes faits
Dans nos enfants et l'amour qu'on leur a donné

Je peux lire dans ton sourire
Les matins où je voudrais en semer plus
Les soirées où je voudrais y voir fleurir un rire coquin

Tu te fais timide et éteins les lumières
Mais ma chère, mes yeux connaissent trop bien l'obscurité
Et toi tu brilles de mille feux à mes yeux

Tu m'en veux car je sais taire ta rage
Je sais soulager ta peine
Je peux atténuer ta migraine
Je sais comment panser tes plaies

Mais tu t'entêtes, et tu sautes
Tête première, à peine remise de la dernière tempête

Je sais ce que tu penses.
Tu t'en veux car je te connais à présent
Et tu pressens les moments
Où je te lis tel un livre ouvert
Mais tu sais au moins
Que je ne m'arrête pas qu'à la couverture.
Tu sais que j'entre le lis de ta rivière.
Tu sais que je baigne dans toutes tes couleurs.
Tu sais que je ne vis que dans ta chaleur

Le constat (desseins malgré le destin)

Il suffit parfois de cligner des yeux
Pour tout perdre de vue

J'ai menti. J'ai tout écrit.
J'ai tout décrit et puis tant pis.
Je préfère savoir que je m'en souviendrais

Je suis un paradoxe.
Je me contredis tout le temps
Mais je suis un homme de principe

Convaincu de mon antithèse
Je cherche pourtant à faire mes preuves

Je me suis fait à l'incertain, au lendemain.
Je m'attends à tendre la main et à perdre mon chemin
Mais je ne prétends pas connaître mon destin
Ni être prêt pour ce jour-ci et encore moins à la fin

Je me tue à vivre d'une façon
Qui plairait à des gens séduits par la mort

Je ne dors plus que quand il fait noir dans mes idées
Après de longues nuits blanches
Où la fatigue ne met pas fin à mes journées

Quand je ne suis pas bavard et ancré
Dans mes propres idées
Je me retrouve imbibé
D'encre comme un buvard
Et j'atteins mes limites

Je saigne par la rime alors je me soigne

Ma conscience est constamment troublée
Par l'inconsistance de ma capacité
À rester conscient de ma connaissance.
Comme un cancer, j'en sens les fers
Se resserrer sur mes pieds et mes mains jointes
Bien que je me sens hors pair
Lorsque j'opère des opérations éponymes à mon âme

Je le fait avec l'espoir de ne pas me perdre moi-même
Alors que choient et trébuchent
Des milliers dans l'eau et sur la roche

Un peu consterné par le constat sur le comptant manquant
Et le constant déni du déficit
Par ceux à qui je rends des comptes
Je me retrouve à faire le pouce à la même place
Au début d'une impasse
Et je m'impose car je m'expose
Mais j'explose car on ne me comprend jamais
Puisqu'on me méprend toujours

Moi aussi je veux aller plus loin.
Qu'y a-t-il d'anormal à vouloir faire du chemin?
Je n'ai pas les sous pour me rendre dans l'autre ville.
Je ne survivrai pas le parcours entre deux oasis
La chaleur de ce désert est bien trop vile

Ce monde ci, je ne sais pas quoi en faire
Je ne pense qu'à le défaire
Je ne pense pas que c'est l'enfer
Mais je cherche toujours le paradis
Dans un antre, une entrevue, un entre-deux
Où j'entreprends de l'entretenir
Pendant qu'entre-temps j'entrevois de l'entrainer
Dans le guet-apens d'une entremise et d'une entreprise
Basée sur l'entrepôt de quelques entrées

Sect of the slow clap

Ask somebody who knows about the body
Someone used to pouring heart and spirits
Someone who lost their mind
Looking for something worth the find

Each of your breaths is but the breadth
Between silent notes in the gripping music
Playing on the akashic instrument

The melody is but a love story
And you are undoubtedly in it
Right in the middle of its span infinite

Born out of the numerous
Ominous, numinous and luminous
Alongside unspeakable deeds
In the hour of miracles
Marvelling at the profound beauty of life
There is a sect that has sworn
To never let their hands touch
Caught in a slow clap
And an ovation

Maybe I will join them...

Smoke chaser

I had to get moving
Before you got used to
Salty kisses on the sand
Sultry dresses on the stand
Silly men that won't understand
The silly sketches you do by hand
Your strong aversion for that one brand
And your sights on something grand

You pull at my heart and end up pushing my pen
You come to be one with me
But leave me in pieces and in pain

I have always been lucky
Even on my worst days
I am sure I got the best
Out of what life could throw at me

Even you, you were a blessing

The worst part of it all
Is that you left in the middle of a sentence
Now I fill cells with hypotheses
For those words left unsaid are my prison

I aim to steal sparks from the fire
And build my own warmth.
That's why I look out
For smoke rising in the sky

If only flames lasted
As long as you were willing to burn
I would have risen from the ashes again and again
Just to keep us shining forever

+ / _*

With the impetus to my love on hiatus
I started losing sight of something glorious

Now the windows of their souls
Were mere witnesses to the record of my dullness

You truly were the whetstone to my blade

I remember still
Those innocent smiles we shared
I wondered many times
If that was all we needed from one another

Perhaps it was and if not it's a pity.
Still I cannot haste
Or promise a more productive encounter

I was drawn by the image
You put on my mind
As you drew my eyes on you

I could tell I hurt you in another life
You loved me with a vengeance

While shorthanded on my share of luck
Under the suspicions
And the influence of what's above
I got into it
Knowing I was unto something
Knowing you were up to something

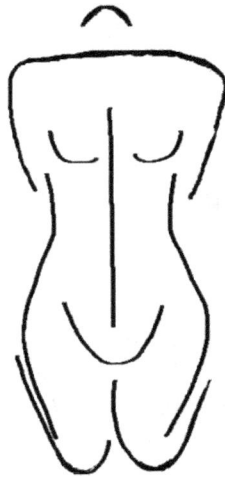

+/-*

To a model for poems

I woke up often with my heart still outside my chest

I have been running all my life
Hoping to run into her
But a mile in her shoes
And I wouldn't make a move

I get cold feet thinking of her warmth.
I second-guess myself even though
She is my first thought of the day
But I inch my way to her each night
As she is my last light
My last thought and my only dream

Making my way through walking nightmares
I followed a dreamy figure
With a bounce in her step

It took an eternity
But I reached the edge of infinity

I reached her

Past countless halves
In the scales of the Ouroboros serpent
I touched her
Who touched me

We were already one
But the test was in the taste of unity

At first we feasted on each other's flesh
Soon we realized we needed more
So we hunted, growing more insatiable

+ / -*

But soon I had to hold back a few inches
In my approach, fearing she wouldn't get it
But my texts, emails and letters grew longer.
I was losing her because I spent too much time
Re-writing everything and stood her up, many times
Because I feared more a misunderstanding
And made too many statements
Attempting to define concepts in the context
In which I would apply in the contest for her heart
The one in her mind
The one I had in mind.
But it was all a dream

Because we haven't met yet
I start imagining
Which strangers she is
And I discover which ones
I wish are not her

And I mix a sigh with a plea:
Please, don't move.
I am still writing
A few verses about you

To thee (thine)

Though I thought it was tough
I saw through it
Through tortuous and thorough thinking

The turnout is my sudden kinship with the ocean.
Caught in the tumultuous waves
I catch breaths in its troughs

In the middle of a school of trouts on a rout
I started touting my doubts
On a rampage that ended my tour

Throughout my short life
I met many with whom I lost touch
The idea, with gloom, doesn't do much
But increase the throughput of memories
That took me only insofar
As to grow a tumour
That weighs heavy
While I still see the humour
Of losing you who lost me

We never had each other
And all we gave to one another
We took back

Or so I thought
Because my heart is still with you
My heart still goes to you

+ / -*

We could make it

J'étais nu devant toi et tu m'as couvert de ta joie
Tu as étouffé ma colère sans voix
Et ramené la chaleur d'autrefois
Et c'est là que j'ai su que l'on ferait tout, dès le début :
L'amour à l'endroit, l'amour à l'envers
L'amour sans réserves, l'amour à moitié
L'amour que l'on craint, l'amour que l'on espère
L'amour sans cœur, l'amour sincère
L'amour dans le noir, l'amour au soleil
L'amour sans surprises, l'amour sans pareil
L'amour sans futur, l'amour sans passé
L'amour quelque fois, l'amour sans s'en passer
L'amour sans un lit, l'amour sans un toit
L'amour sans s'unir, l'amour sans toi

Par contre

Comme inscrit sur une pièce contre plaquée
Surmontant un bout de terre me servant de dernier carré
Mon contre-espionnage m'a amené
À contrecœur et contre la volonté du ciel
À voguer à contre-courant et contre le vent

C'était un contretemps
Un peu contre nature et contre toute attente
Mais je cours toujours contre la montre.
Par contre, bien que contre-indiqué
Dans un contre-interrogatoire
J'ai contre-attaqué pour contrebalancer le mal déjà fait
Mais je m'en contre-fiche, je suis la règle des contre-exemples

The jackpot

Digital wordplay foreplay preludes
Coordinates and time estimations
Body language, projection and translations
Crude nude the prude would occlude
Until the increase in altitude concludes
And finally nothing precludes being in touch with negritude

I stretch my reach up to her updo
But that definitely won't do
So I grab both of her arms locked behind her back
While she moans increasingly louder
Every word but our password, our safe word

Attempting to make it last forever, I draw her silhouette
Embossed in the path taken by the dripping sweat
Following the curves of her fishnet
Torn in the one spot where the tearing won't stop

She's the kind of person
That stays with you long after they left
So I sink in my memory of her
Again and again to recollect
Every detail, every moment
All that she left on my mind
All that I felt with my body

If I met her by chance
Then by now I am out luck

With tenderness aforethought (Penelope, Venus of Negus)

The good times are clear as day

She rang and I looked at what she brought
I always knew there might come some time
For her to bring herself to end it
In the meantime I would be running out of steam
Before I run out of time

Following faithful footfalls going upstairs
The bed was sliding on the ceramic floor of the apartment
It turned into the cyclic rhythm of a bedpost
Hitting into the wall in the same spots
Like young lovers carving their names on the bark of a tree

We engaged in the appraisal of gadgetry
Until we were groggy
We went at it with a grudge
But I won't let you be the judge
Of fair play in foreplay or swordplay

Often adorned with lazuli, she was gorgeous
And she permeated the air
With the scent of lilac and nectarine

She was a closed bud of a lotus flower sitting in mud
The unheard echo of a forgotten hollow dud

She was wayward with a lifeline
That was anything but lifelike

She was thirsty for fulfilment from fruitful endeavours
She was ferocious and voracious

+/-*

She had a rare rearing with rigorous revering for reveries
That would make her at times roar
Growing a halo with her aura
Arching her back like a dark wolf
Drawn under the light of a distant aurora

She was a proponent
Of a thesis on catharsis
Status and stasis

But the hands of time slowly stretched
Further than the circumference of the clock
They reached up to her face and pulled
Snatching her smile off

Believing she would turn fifty
Because she was close to her first quarter of a century
She feared of one day ending up vegetative
To be caught in the lifelong loophole
To the original sin without become a saint

The very thought made her vivid

It was a shock, something chronic
Had taken root but she chuckled
Thinking of going full circle
On going back to church
But there was something cynical
About how she was visiting clinic after clinic

But it wasn't all about her fears
It was mostly about her dreams

We clicked quickly
And fatally, we fell for one another.
It was more than a fling

+/-*

Our fateful encounter
Happened when I was but fifteen.
We met in the unfair season of summer, by the fair
And soon we were catching unsuspecting Finnish finfish
Running at the bend of the river for the finish

Amid the sound of norias working through the night
We ran on the hill as if we were wearing talarias
Disturbing swarms of fireflies
Until we fell on our backs
Squinting our eyes
Trying to find maria on the moon
Until they closed in the hope
That the next day wouldn't come so soon

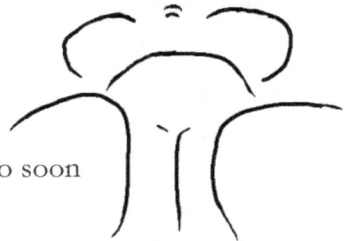

Behind those concave cavities
Where complicated but concrete
Abstract notions would become realities
That at times clashed with the views of the complacent
Which were easier to believe
And distribute through entertainment
Inconspicuously but not without consequence
We connected subconsciously

There was no coincidence
And soon it would be the time for our bodies to dance

Our first time was after a concert
Drowning in the melody of classic music from a Cadillac.
I recall her floriferous landscape
The fluff in her bosom
The transpiration and the trepidation

Subtle motion akin to Gaussian blur
Applies in the distance to background noise
And the colors of the backdrop

+/-*

Tactile memory brings me back
To intimate and kinky handshakes
In a household of piping hot late meals and treats
With portions in the right proportions

Sometimes on long travels where I would get carsick
I would shuffle through mementos
In the words of memos
Bunched up in a memoir
She had memorized

Something that she wanted read
At her memorial
In her memory
At the foot of her monument
A tribute made with all her attributes in mind
That she felt was a token totem
But still a quick ticket
To her next destination

We became distant in the gulf of an instant.
Out of nowhere she concluded
That love was but an unreachable catchall try-catch contraption
That could contradict itself through conviction
And was always in direct conflict with conventions
A trap for suckers
That hoped she knew better because she did better
And engaged with her in casuistic exchange

It was already comical that the chemical
Would become cosmic simply because we didn't grasp it
Even if we found ourselves prisoners of its wirework
And the titillation in our heads
From stardust fireworks

+/-*

She canceled our future
By putting it on hold
And like the cur I was
Somehow I concurred
And she went on to conquer
The rest of the herd
The rest of the world

Later I learned that it was because
There was blood in the water of the river
And there at the edge of the cataract
Was brooding a catastrophe

Around that time many others left
Bamboozled by the babbling
Bulbs colored by the bloodbath
That soaked the land
Where were sown bullets, dirty bombs and mines
Bought and brought thanks to bribes
In a hotbed for conflicts
Untamed regions showing on maps
As a tessellated patchwork of calico cat colours
Suiting barren wastelands and Thanatos

Though misnamed
In the last moment
She went ahead with her misnomer
That was her chance for the life of another

It was a cinch
Thanks to mnemonic techniques
She metamorphosed
Mimicking her new image

She was a copycat
Who had conveniently overheard a covenant

+/-*

Convincingly and elegantly enunciated
The concept was a clever plot
A contract made between convicts
Coerced into acting civic
In the middle of a circus
Where all that was missing was cosmetic

As the recipient of myriad proclamations of adoration
She was a percipient wielder of power

She played her character well
She said she was practicing celibacy
In a chaotic time for matrimony

As if she had clairvoyance
She would circumvent any questions
That would shed her guise
Concealing what she couldn't concede
And as they inched forward she'd recede

She started deluding herself
Believing their divisive discredit
Could dilute her worth

Even though she was clad with an advanced caducous armor
She got greedy and capricious
And as capacious as she got vacuous

Looking to be vindicated and avenged fivefold
With a fistful of hatred
She started scheming to belittle her adversaries
Through poor and egregious schesis
Depending on a defense
Against the offense
Of an unjust sentence

+/_*

But with the circumstances circa that era
Her case was made out to be hysteria
In a paper popular to paupers made of the populace
That she saw as traitors and opponents
And for whom she felt disdain

She fell to a bottomless precipice
Preoccupied because she was unprepared
She brought forth a proposition
A posit that would assure her position
With the proper promise to be propelled even higher

She concocted what she thought to be a foolproof plan
And forcefully went for it
She couldn't declare defeat
She couldn't forfeit this life

The tension grew stronger
As opposing factions gained traction
In a deadly deadlock deducted from that deciding decade

Her ace in the hole was an age of ice and ash
Preluded by one last ebb
An act added to her play for allies
That would pursue her follies

. . .

Were we meant to live this long
Although we don't know how
Or what to do in the meanwhile?

While upfront we stand right in the middle
Of a strange shame that rose to level up to our lips
And like raindrops dancing atop the surface
Of water already overflowing at the brim

+/-*

She poured one too many ideas out of me
She brought out a lot, even the worst

As barbaric as gargoyles look like
They are probably the true form of angels

...

Though missing analogies from our dialogues in a secret dialect
I write this elegy before I write any eulogy
An aporia in the depiction of a utopia
Stated in the euphoria of nostalgia

And as with the tradition of transition in transformations
Trials and tribulations come together
With halted permanence and constancy
In the transaction of transmigrations

Meaning gets lost in translation
Words get lost in transmission and transcription
So now I use tetration to describe uncharted territory
Transpositions of transducers
In the synergy of different energies
Unholy but unworldly transfigurations
And trisection through truncation
And transgressions committed
Through transcendence and transmutation

...

I could blame it on my proclivity for protracted pedantry
But I wrote about her longer than we were together
Longer than we knew each other
Because at some point we lived within forever

•·•·•·•·•·•·•·•·•·•·•·•·•

+ / -*

.
.
.
.
.
.
.
.
.
.

Scribere est loqui at loqui non est scribere.

+ / -*

It was hard for me to pick a title.
I feel like there cannot only be one.

C'était dur pour moi de choisir un titre.
Je pense qu'il ne peut pas y en avoir qu'un.

Voici les autres noms que j'attribue à cette collection :
Here are the other names I give to this selection:

- Négritude et Présence Africaine
- The Negus is a Star
- Abstract on concrete
- Projet Prométhé
- La grande heure de la folie
- Strokes of a poet's portraits
- Eclectic esthetics and evocative emissives
- Death's deep kiss
- La profondeur des plus hauts sommets
- Oblong faces in volume
- L'acte de se désoeuvrer
- Suicide note continued

Other poetry collections: Colourful Citations and sub-collections «Accounts of Withdrawal» (poems in English) and «Sommaire du Fanstaque» (poems in French).

Autres recueils : Colourful Citations et les sous-receuils «Accounts of Withdrawal» (poèmes en anglais) et «Sommaire du Fantasque» (poèmes en français).

www.ingramcontent.com/pod-product-compliance
Lightning Source LLC
Chambersburg PA
CBHW060327050426
42449CB00011B/2685